VILLAGES IN CITIES

Dedicated to Lucia Kowaluk,

community organizer extraordinaire

VILLAGES IN CITIES

Community Land Ownership, Co-operative Housing, and the Milton-Parc Story

JOSHUA HAWLEY

DIMITRIOS ROUSSOPOULOS

Editors

Montreal • New York • Chicago • London

Copyright ©2019 Black Rose Books
Second printing

No part of this book may be reproduced or transmitted in any form, by any means electronic or mechanical including photocopying and recording, or by any information storage or retrieval system – without written permission from the publisher, or, in the case of photocopying or other reprographic copying, a license from the Canadian Copyright Licensing Agency, Access Copyright, with the exception of brief passages quoted by a reviewer in a newspaper or magazine.

Black Rose Books No. SS398

Library and Archives Canada Cataloguing in Publication

    Villages in cities / Josh Hawley and Dimitrios Roussopoulos, editors.

Issued in print and electronic formats.
ISBN 978-1-55164-688-6 .–ISBN 978-1-55164-687-9
–ISBN 978-1-55164-689-3

    1. Housing–Canada–Case studies. 2. Housing, Cooperative–Canada–Case studies. 3. Land trusts–Canada–Case studies. 4. Right to housing–Canada–Case studies. 5. Housing–United States–Case studies. 6. Housing, Cooperative–United States–Case studies. 7. Land tenure–United States–Case studies. 8. Right to housing–United States–Case studies. 9. Case studies.
I. Roussopoulos, Dimitrios I., editor II. Hawley, Josh, 1988-, editor

HD7287.72.C3V55 2018   307.3'360971   C2018-906180-4
                                                                   C2018-906181-2

C.P. 35788 Succ. Léo Pariseau
Montréal, QC H2X 0A4
CANADA
www.blackrosebooks.com

ORDERING INFORMATION

USA/INTERNATIONAL	CANADA	UK/EUROPE
University of Chicago Press Chicago Distribution Center 11030 South Langley Avenue Chicago IL 60628	University of Toronto Press 5201 Dufferin Street Toronto, ON M3H 5T8	Central Books Freshwater Road Dagenham RM8 1RX
(800) 621-2736 (USA) (773) 702-7000 (International) orders@press.uchicago.edu	1-800-565-9523 utpbooks@utpress.utoronto.ca	+44 20 8525 8800 contactus@centralbooks.com

Black Rose Books is the publishing project of Cercle Noir et Rouge

Contents

6 Acknowledgements

8 Introduction
    Joshua Hawley and Dimitrios Roussopoulos

18 *January 1971 MPCC Introductory Pamphlet*

24 Milton-Parc: How We Did It and How It Works Now
    Lucia Kowaluk and Carolle Piché-Burton

36 *1969 Free Press*

39 Champlain Housing Trust
    Brenda Torpy

51 *1970 Architecture Canada Newsmagazine Debate*

55 Montreal and Boston: Intertwined Destinies
    Julien Deschênes

66 *Spring-Summer 1971* BULLDOZER: *Bulletin of the MPCC*

72 *1972 Community Press (formerly the* BULLDOZER*)*

83 On Housing
    Lucia Kowaluk

91   *1973 Arrests and Trial*

98   Housing Co-ops: Citizen Control or Social Service
     Joshua Hawley

108 *1979 Letter from Lucia Kowaluk to Phyllis Lambert and Heritage Montreal*

122 Social Production of Housing
     Iman Salama

130 *1983 CMHC Press Release on the Inauguration of Milton-Parc*

134 Interview with Dimitrios Roussopoulos

146 Interview with Lucia Kowaluk

155 Appendix A: Financial and Technical Participation of CMHC in Milton-Parc

157 Appendix B: Timeline of Milton-Parc: 1979-1987

162 About the authors

Acknowledgements

THIS BOOK WOULD not have been possible without full access to the Milton-Parc archives housed at the Canadian Centre for Architecture. Thank you to all the CCA staff who helped us navigate through this huge depository and to John Goedike for spending hours pouring over the documents and photos and bringing history alive with his anecdotes. Thank you to Robert Cohen for the fascinating discussions on Milton-Parc. Thank you to Phoebe Munro and Peter Mathewson for their thorough and thoughtful edits to this book. A million thanks to the residents of Milton-Parc, whose passion for their neighbourhood is an inspiration to defend and build the power of working class neighbourhoods everywhere.

Finally, we recall history and the valiant and courageous militancy of the Milton-Parc Citizens Committee, without which the Milton-Parc project would have been impossible; and to the wonderful 59 arrestees who confronted Concordia Estates Ltd in their offices and got justice when they won their trial.

Introduction

Joshua Hawley and Dimitrios Roussopoulos

> *"Milton-Parc is also much more—it is people, people getting together in their search for a better community within the larger one. A village within the city."*
> —Anonymous, *Let Me Talk to You About Milton-Parc*, circa 1983

LIKE POLLUTION, gentrification cannot be contained by borders. A pollutant may emanate from one source but it spreads from farmland to river, from exhaust pipe to air, from city to ocean, affecting species and habitats along the way. Likewise, a city or neighbourhood in the midst of an influx of finance capital and *en vogue* speculation may be the emitter of toxic "urban renewal," "beautification," and "liveability," but the displacement of people from their homes has effects that cross neighbourhood and municipal boundaries.

Diluting the effects of gentrification through inclusionary zoning—the offsetting of total displacement by sprinkling a token amount of so-called affordable housing in among "resort-style" apartment or luxury condo complexes—presupposes that residential and commercial real estate developers, speculative investors, and urban planners have the right to control and shape our cities and neighbourhoods. These corporate interest groups are driven by profit and an ingrained sense of technocratic superiority, like the urban planners who see themselves as innovators and "community designers," turning neighbourhoods freshly vacated of poor people into their sandboxes. Their continued legitimacy in determining the future of cities crushes the opportunity for people with lower incomes to build their own lives and destroys the interpersonal networks that make up the social phenomenon that is a city.

This book presents a different kind of solution to the question of urban land, one that's been implemented in cities around the world, not under one banner or movement, but under a common militant belief that the only way to secure housing and prevent people from being forcibly evicted or priced out of their homes is to decommodify the land. Through various strategies and mechanisms, land that is taken off the real estate market is protected from speculation. This becomes a common heritage which inevitably develops into a sense of community and citizenship.

Land ownership has always been central in questions of economic development, justice, and equality. It was Jean-Jacques Rousseau who wrote in 1775, "Beware of listening to the imposter; you are undone if you once forget that the fruits of the earth belong to us all, and the earth itself to nobody." Or Adam Smith who a year later, in 1776, wrote: "Civil government, so far as it is instituted for the security of property, is, in reality, instituted for the defence of the rich against the poor, or those who have property against those who have none at all." Or again Joseph Stiglitz who, in 2015, wrote "Much of the growth in inequality and the increase in the wealth-income ratio are related to an increase in rent and land values." The nature of the urban economy—who owns it and who controls it—is up for intense scrutiny, and we need to set more ambitious goals in our striving for economic democracy.

This book focuses on the need for community land trusts, especially in urban centres, to protect land and housing from capitalist extraction and speculation. Such land, permanently in the hands of community control, forms the base on which to develop community-led social housing, economic development, and ecological transformation. These are the villages in cities that we urgently need to transform our society. Indeed, they are already being created.

Only once land is removed from market forces, not just free from speculation, can our homes actually be considered decommodified. Non-profit, co-operative housing doesn't accomplish this on its own. Everything in the process to develop this housing has been commodified, from the stolen, unceded indigenous land to the extracted raw materials to the construction workers exploited by private companies. Removing profit at the source of provision doesn't erase its exploitative lifecycle, let alone the fact that non-profit landlords, whether they be staffed or self-managed, still collect rent and evict tenants.

Resident/citizen-led projects that aim to decommodify the land—to free the land from market forces—remain concretely focused on their implicit anti-capitalist goal, as opposed to institutionalized organizations which tend to prioritize promoting their sector's workforce of non-profit service providers. The international co-operative movement, for example, has an institutionalized corporate structure and its own rule book which has become abstracted to the point of being co-opted by the existing power structure. This is not unlike much of the trade union movement. Even the co-op stalwart Mondragon, headquartered in the Basque region of Spain, has a number of subsidiaries in China which are practically indistinguishable from regular multinationals which have created a hybrid, "co-opitalist" enterprise.[1] There is an irony herein. Both the co-operative and trade union movements have a crying need for renewal. The stakes are high, in both cases. Consider the impact of the co-operative movement on the global economy—worldwide, the co-op movement employs more than 100 million people and counts nearly one billion people as members.²

With regard to the non-profit co-operative housing sector, it is still largely at the mercy of the politics of city governments and the capitalist driven real estate industry that celebrates profit before life itself. Add to this the drama that urban real estate is very much the preferred investment choice of finance capital, the consequence of which is that entire neighbourhoods have been hollowed out to make way for condos and "multi-use" office buildings with built-in hotels and apartments. Nothing stands in the way of this massive wave of urbanization except citizens—organized citizens. And at the top of the agenda is who should own and control urban land.

Milton-Parc and the Community Land Trust Movement

The closest efforts to decommodify urban land in North America (perhaps even in the Global North) have come from the community land trust (CLT) model. The CLT is an American creation, with New Communities Inc. in Georgia being credited as the first. New Communities Inc., born out of the Civil Rights Movement, became the largest African American co-operative farm of its time.³ Land is held in trust, not solely for conservation purposes, but for the land's use value, laying the foundation for self-determination.

Since then, a multitude of creative interventions have been used to establish CLTs, each specific to the political, cultural, and economic circumstances of its time, such as the Caño Martín Peña Community Land Trust in San Juan, Puerto Rico, which is a CLT formed by residents of squatter settlements along a polluted waterway, or the flurry of activity to decommodify land around the Bay Area, California.

Then there is the Communauté Milton Parc (CMP) in Montreal, a remarkable project that will form a central focus of this book. The CMP is based on the uniquely innovative legal framework "condominium for social purposes" where the condo members are not individual residents but 22 community-run non-profit corporations—15 housing co-ops, six non-profit housing projects, and the Société de Développement Communautaire Milton-Parc (SDC), which runs the commercial properties. The CMP, created through a private member's bill at the Quebec National Assembly in 1987, has been able to abolish speculation over six contiguous downtown blocks through its rock-solid Declaration of Co-ownership which effectively prevents the buying and selling of property as well as instituting strict socio-economic criteria in the process of selecting new members to favor very low and low-income people.

The Milton-Parc struggle was initiated in the sixties when a "developer" started buying up a six-block area, building by building, with the intention of destroying the neighbourhood through processes of "urban renewal"; their strategies included running homes into the ground, displacing tenants through slum conditions and evictions, demolishing quality homes in order to build "the city of the twenty-first century," and pricing tenants out through the modernist logic of gentrification. From its founding in the turbulent year of 1968, the Milton-Parc Citizens' Committee (MPCC-CCMP) wanted to abolish speculation, stop gentrification, preserve their neighbourhood and its architecture, improve living conditions, and defend their territory against future attacks by "developers". They sought early on to build common strength, grassroots power, and resilience among residents. They worked to control their future and avoid the commodification of their housing which outside economic and political interests tried to impose on them.

The MPCC always embraced the idea that its mission was much more than just saving buildings. It was more than a battle to protect housing for low-income people and to save heritage greystone Victorian buildings—the struggle was also to generate a community based on a co-operative idea. The housing project was built from the ground up through countless hours of door-knocking, face-to-face meetings, and debate. This movement did involve the input and guidance of many professionals, who in turn always understood that this was a resident-led movement and, once established, the residents would ultimately assume control. As described by one of the lead professionals involved, Robert Cohen: "There is no other non-speculative, non-profit project like this one in Canada. It's a community running itself."[4] This vision of resident/citizen control of their neighbourhood, not as a non-profit for the professional, managerial class, but as a working class, "citizens' corporation," first coalesced as an alternative plan from a Community Design Workshop held in September 1971. This was well before that vision was formalized in 1980 with the Action Plan that laid out the structure and organization that would eventually become the Communauté Milton-Parc (CMP) land trust.

Published for the 30th anniversary of the CMP and the 50th anniversary of the citizens' committee, this book originally emerged to commemorate this history of political struggle and community organizing. It goes further to explore the principles of the community control of land and housing in connection with other case studies in North America. The book is compiled from three sources. First, there are contributions from authors on the history and functioning of various CLTs, the social production of habitat, and the co-op movement. Second, interspersed between these are historical documents from the Milton-Parc archives housed at the Canadian Centre for Architecture (CCA) in Montreal.[5] Finally, the book ends with interviews with two long-time Milton-Parc residents, organizers, founding members of the MPCC, and life partners—Lucia Kowaluk and Dimitrios Roussopoulos.[6]

* * *

In the last five years, housing prices in Oakland, only ten minutes by transit from notoriously expensive San Francisco, have doubled and median rents have risen by $1,000. The city has lost around 30% of its Black population since 2000.[7] You can't travel far without passing an established tent city, some of which even operate on co-operative values. This is a city in the midst of massive displacement of the poor and people of colour.

The grassroots organizing around these issues in and around Oakland is impressive. Under the Bay Area Consortium of Community Land Trusts, there are: the Bay Area Community Land Trust, Housing Land Trust of Sonoma County, the Northern California Land Trust, San Francisco Community Land Trust, the Community Land Trust of West Marin, Oakland CLT, and Preserving Affordable Housing Assets Longterm, Inc. of East Palo Alto.[8] These organizations have been effective at taking land off the capitalist market, plot-by-plot. This has happened through different means, such as private donations or by convincing autonomous housing co-ops to join. For example, Fairview House in Berkeley, an intentional community started by a group of anarchist students in the 1960s, "entered into a relationship with the Northern California Land Trust that sets income limits on new members" in order to maintain affordability and "freedom from the speculative real estate market."[9]

Oakland, then, seemed an appropriate place for a gathering of people fighting for decommodified housing and land during the 2017 conference of Grounded Solutions Network, the American network of CLTs. At both the Oakland conference and the 2018 national conference in Pittsburgh, there was a Canadian delegation. Among the delegation were longstanding and emerging Canadian urban land trust groups, which see community ownership of land and the development of housing as the way to reclaim neighbourhoods. From Vancouver is Hogan's Alley Trust, intent on reclaiming the anchor neighbourhood for the city's Black population which was deliberately destroyed by the municipal government through tactics of "revitalization." In Toronto, the Parkdale Neighbourhood Land Trust is working to protect ever-disappearing rooming houses and scoop up land to develop non-profit housing and community spaces in one of the city centre's last working-class neighbourhoods. So far, they've managed to acquire the Milky Way Garden, a 7,000 square feet vacant property turned community garden, and also their first residential building, a rooming house threatened by displacement. And of course there is the Communauté Milton-Parc (CMP) and Milton-Parc Citizens' Committee (MPCC-CCMP) from Montréal.

With CLTs catching on in Canada, evidenced by the number of groups emerging in the last few years, there was agreement amongst the Canadian delegation at the two U.S. conferences that removing urban land from the speculative market and turning it over to collective, community ownership should only be pursued while considering how to end the legitimating of colonial control of unceded Indigenous territory. This was determined to be a long-term goal, but one that must be articulated from the outset of any community land acquisition project.

Curiously, in the United States, CLTs have major backing from financial juggernauts and accomplished predatory lenders, Wells Fargo and JPMorgan Chase. At this point, it's unclear whether the banks support CLTs as a form of socially responsible investment (SRI), as public relations penance for the 2008 housing crisis, or as a move to co-opt and undermine an effective tool to ensure permanent affordability of housing. Whatever the reason for their support, the corporate finance and non-profit presence at the conference, although highly visible, was overwhelmed by the sheer number and enthusiasm of grassroots organizers who spend their lives fighting developers and city governments that expel all but the rich, pushing people of colour and the poor beyond their financial and emotional limits—and beyond the geographic limits of the city.

Despite a "best practices" orientation inevitably emerging from the institutionalization of a movement, grassroots urban land trusts around the world demonstrate there is not one single model to follow. Although "single-family homes on collectively-owned land" is the default CLT model promoted by Grounded Solutions Network, there is a lot of talk of how resident-run housing—co-op housing—shares the same values and goals of CLTs. Many CLTs have already taken this approach. However, others remain open to private home-ownership to broaden their prospects for funding in the interest of acquiring as much land as possible.

CLTs have been shown to be an effective tool in protecting land and creating lasting housing for low-income people. From the Champlain Housing Trust in Burlington, Vermont, whose founders turned to Milton-Parc for inspiration over 30 years ago, to the UK's National CLT Network, which grew from 30 CLTs in 2010 to over 200 in 2017,[10] community organizers have begun normalizing the idea and practice of urban residents collectively controlling the land they live on in.

CLTs, the Neighbourhood, and the City

Clearly, the ownership of land—urban land specifically—has become an issue of growing importance in the minds of organizers in social movements that focus on housing, poverty, and quality of life matters. The absolute right to private property regarding land and its ownership is now being questioned and alternatives are being sought.

However, in Canada, the Canada Mortgage and Housing Corporation still elevates private home ownership as the ultimate solution. They view housing as a continuum. On one end is homelessness. Next to this is supportive housing, followed by social housing, co-ops and non-profits, market rent, and finally private homeownership. According to the State, Canadians are eager to pay mortgages.

How are tenants, especially poor ones, expected to build a sense of community if their homes are considered only gateways to private ownership? Communities are strengthened through rootedness and strong communities are foundational to a meaningful democracy. Shouldn't low-income housing be considered more than just transitional? Urban land trusts may be the tool needed to create low-income housing that is socially cohesive, empowered, and deeply rooted for the long-term.

The need for community control goes beyond the question of housing, but touches on the very issues at the heart of our cities. There is growing recognition that cities are held back from becoming more egalitarian and free by corporate greed, loss of public space, and rising inequality. Across the world, urban reformers and urban radicals are putting urban ecology into practice, transforming abandoned public spaces, setting up community co-operatives, and powering up citizen engagement in public affairs.

Building inclusive and equitable local economies requires a fair redistribution of wealth and ensuring the poor benefit from urban improvement efforts. What is equally important is an equitable redistribution of decision-making power, involving participatory planning and democratic participation over how neighbourhoods should develop and how local economic resources are allocated. The cry for community control is becoming louder again.

As the debate unfolds, the larger dimension of the municipalization of the urban economy appears on the political horizon. This is distinguished from "nationalization" which leads to bureaucratic and top-down control. Municipalization insists on the idea that all land should be public municipal land and democratically accountable to the local community. What is constructed on top of that land can be owned by different organizations—private, co-operative, or non-profit—but the ultimate objective is to render the land of an entire city under public ownership and managed by the city government in partnership with community organizations and land trusts of various sizes and vocations. The municipality—or, more precisely, the citizen body grounded in face-to-face assembly—absorbs the economy as an aspect of public business, and no longer a realm privatized for self-serving enterprises. Thus the debate beyond the community land trust has been engaged.

In Quebec, this visionary political objective has a history. François Saillant, (perhaps the most famous tenant rights activist in Quebec), in his 2018 book *Lutter pour un toit*, notes in his conclusion that three Quebec political parties in the 1970s proposed the elimination of land speculation by the "progressive municipalization of urban land." The *Front d'action politique* (FRAP: the acronym is French for hit) was a radical political party formed out of an alliance of citizen organizations and labour unions in the late 1960s. Its political descendant was the *Rassemblement des citoyens et des citoyennes de Montréal* (the Montreal Citizens' Movement, RCM-MCM), a political party founded to contest the authoritarian rule of the then Mayor Jean Drapeau and his handpicked candidates. Both the FRAP and the RCM were quite popular, the latter even winning 18 city council seats in its first election of 1974 before later winning the mayoralty. In addition, the separatist provincial party, the *Parti québécois* (PQ), also advocated for the municipalization of urban land. With these three grassroots political parties, municipalization was put on the political agenda.

The More Things Change
The archival materials in this book celebrate the Milton-Parc Citizens' Committee's grounding in the historical working-class struggle over housing. The organizational capacity of the tenants and the phenomenal amount of labour they put in, as well as the vivacity of the surrounding discourse, comes alive through excerpts from self-published community newspapers, correspondence letters, newspaper articles, and op-eds. The propaganda put out by the MPCC during its decade of protest was highly charged, informed, and co-ordinated. It reflects the political militancy of the residents and their strategy of direct action against organized capital—politicians, developers, investors, banks, and the police. The archival materials in this book acts as a guide for organizers who face similar struggles. What's remarkable is that they are as relevant today as they were 50 years ago. They draw a concrete link between current struggles and the Milton-Parc Citizens' Committee's approach from 1968 to 1972.

The ongoing battle to save our neighbourhoods has been taken up by groups such as Parkdale: Organize! in Toronto, Hamilton Tenants Solidarity Network (HTSN), and Herongate Tenant Coalition (HTC)[11] in Ottawa. These groups see that the most immediate way to defend our homes and communities is not by defaulting to the non-profit sector, but by building independent working-class neighbourhood power and directly confronting those who extract profit from us, in particular landlords. Since the summer of 2017, Parkdale: Organize! has undertaken two successful mass rent strikes in apartment buildings, forcing landlords to drop rent increases and do much-needed repairs. HTSN has put direct pressure on landlords and won material improvements in tenants' lives, such as repairs and increasing the heat in the winter.

HTC has launched what is likely the largest housing rights case ever heard in Canada after over 500 Black and Brown tenants were evicted from their homes in Herongate in the summer of 2018 so the landlord can attract a whiter, more affluent tenant base. Herongate, a largely family-oriented working-class neighbourhood in the south end of Canada's capital, Ottawa, is experiencing a profound redevelopment. The landlord, Toronto-based Timbercreek Asset Management, is now constructing "resort-style apartments" where the demolished homes once sat. Leilani Farha, the United Nations Special Rapporteur on Adequate Housing, who lives in Ottawa, has called these evictions an "egregious violation of human rights."

The Herongate Tenant Coalition has been directly inspired by the historical precedent set by the MPCC beginning in 1968. The language used by the MPCC in their battle against Concordia Estates Ltd. (the company that wanted to destroy Milton-Parc) can be used interchangeably with urban battles now underway. Take, for example, the following passage from the MPCC's 1971 community newspaper. Changing only a few words reveals how little has changed:

> If we cannot stop Concordia [Timbercreek], the people who live in Milton-Park [Herongate] will have to leave. A community will be destroyed. And people like them—immigrant, French-Canadian [working class, Muslim], low-income, and families—will not replace them. But the rich, unmarried or childless, the passing student, the professional on their way to the suburbs, will climb up to their bachelor apartment, and look down on what used to be a neighbourhood.

The parallels are uncanny. The more things change, the more they stay the same.

The authors' contributions to this book tie the Milton-Parc struggle to global examples of self-determination through community ownership of urban land and co-op housing—collective efforts to counter the destructive force of capitalism on the people who live in cities. The value of these chapters lies not in blind hope and optimism but in the visions of alternatives to the dominant, mainstream urban order of control, and in the critical lens through which these alternatives are viewed. The new world that we want to create is already being developed everyday, everywhere. Our battles are similar, and our work for social change is part of a historical process that began long before us and will continue long after. And so we need to learn from each other and from those who have gone before us, take inspiration from our successes and challenges, and build solidarity across our movements. Hopefully, this book will be an important contribution to this.

EDITORS' NOTE

Spelling has been left untouched in the archival materials, except for a few minor grammar or typo corrections. Throughout the struggle, Milton-Parc was spelled

primarily as Milton-Park, especially in English documents. Over the years, the French spelling has become the norm, both in English and French usage. "Citizen" is used throughout this book not in the nationalist sense of a person who is "a legally recognized subject or national of a state," but as a resident of a city.
The interviews have been edited for clarity, readability, and factual correctness.

REFERENCES

Allen-Price, Olivia. 2017. 'How Many Are Being Displaced by Gentrification in Oakland?' KQED. 9 February 2017. https://bit.ly/2XQca4o.

Askew, Kate, '*Alliance coopérative internationale,* and *Année internationale des coopératives.*' 2012. *Building a Better World: 100 Stories of Co-operation.*

Focus; [Geneva: Sydney, Australia; International Co-operative Alliance.

Errasti, Anjel. 2015. 'Mondragon's Chinese Subsidiaries: Coopitalist Multinationals in Practice.' *Economic and Industrial Democracy* 36 (3): 479–99. https://doi.org/10.1177/0143831X13511503.

Helman, Claire. 1987. *The Milton-Park Affair: Canada's Largest Citizen-Developer Confrontation.* Montréal: Véhicule Press.

Napier, Joyce. 1983. 'Party Celebrates Rescue of a Neighbourhood.' *The Globe and Mail,* 26 September 1983.

NOTES
1 Errasti, 2015.
2 Askey, 2012.
3 See the documentary Arc of Justice, 2016 www.arcofjusticefilm.com
4 Napier, 1983. Statement by Robert Cohen, the executive director of the Milton-Parc Technical Resource Group, during the inauguration of Milton-Parc in 1983. Quoted in *The Globe and Mail.*
5 The CCA was founded by philanthropist architect Phyllis Lambert, who was instrumental in helping the residents of Milton-Parc realize their project and persuading the federal government to financially back it.
6 So many people were involved in the citizen struggle to save Milton-Parc, and unfortunately not all of their stories can be included here. *The Milton-Parc Story,* a history of the neighbourhood from multiple perspectives by Joshua Hawley, will soon be available online.
7 Allen-Price, 2017.
8 www.bacclt.org
9 www.fairviewhouse.org
10 www.communitylandtrusts.org.uk/what-is-a-clt/about-clts
11 https://herongatetenants.ca/

January 1971
MPCC Introductory Pamphlet

Introductory Pamphlet

Why — does the Milton-Park Association exist?

Because — Montreal has a housing problem that is steadily getting worse:

— while prices climb steadily, 30% of Montreal is poor, existing on incomes that are fixed, or which, in the past ten years have been outpaced by inflation.

— although the number of poor is increasing, all new houses being built are designed for highest profit. Without exception, they are out of reach of those Montrealers who most desperately need new homes.

— even those houses that the poor now live in are being taken from them. 25,000 low income housing units have been replaced by commercial projects, highways, and many many parking lots.

— city tax policies make it more attractive to landlords to allow their properties to fall into disrepair, to sell out to "developers," or to just clear the land.

— public housing, because of labour and material costs, is enormously expensive. The City of Montreal has spent its energy on showplace projects, such as Expo, which to the poor, only serve to raise prices.

It is clear that reigning politicians will do nothing to correct this situation. Those in need must fight together for common goals. Only group action can develop housing co-operatives, neighbourhood administered social services, or any other aspect of community control.

Many newcomers to the Milton-Park Committee felt confused by the issues being dealt with in response to this need, we have attempted to present the facts in an organized fashion. We need the help of anyone interested and welcome your suggestions. Meetings are Tuesday nights at 8:00 p.m. at the University settlement at 3553 St. Urbain St.

History Of The Committee

Having started solely as a group opposing the Concordia project, the Milton-Park Citizens' Committee has broadened its scope to include such community projects as a daycare centre for small children, a street festival, and a newspaper, among others.

Summer 1968: tenants and proprietors, living mainly within the six-block area of the projected Concordia plan, having heard that Concordia intended to have the City expropriate those homes which it did not yet possess, held a public meeting. One hundred and sixty-six people attended this meeting.

August 1968: a questionnaire was sent around to the residents of the six-block area. The results are as follows:
1. 92% of the people interviewed gave their support to the citizens' committee.
2. The majority of the residents had lived in the area five years or more, and many have lived in the area for more than 35 years. 97% expressed the desire to remain in the area.
3. A large majority of those polled favoured rehabilitation of present housing, rather than demolition.
4. A large majority of Concordia tenants expressed serious complaints against this landlord. These complaints were about repairs, cleaning, vermin, etc. Only a minimal number of tenants of other landlords had such complaints.

The Milton-Park Citizens' Committee outlined its three major goals:
1. To develop a counter-proposition to the Concordia plan which would favour rehabilitation of the majority of homes.
2. To develop essential community services, such as daycare centres, co-operatives, etc.
3. To protect tenants against abuse and injustice from Concordia such as poor maintenance of the properties and delays in major repairs.

Sept.–Oct.: The Committee met unsuccessfully with Concordia on the question of citizens' participation in their project.

October 1968: The Committee presented a brief to the Hellyer Commission on Housing.

January 1969: The Committee met with M. Alie, the city councillor for this area regarding the mountain-view by-law. This by-law, already in effect to the west of University Street, limits the height of buildings in order to protect the view of Mount Royal. M. Alie encouraged the Committee to follow this up—but that was all.

February 1969: The Committee, not having been invited to a meeting between the City Planning Department and Concordia, in which Concordia's plans for the area were being presented, requested to attend. The city approved, but Concordia's representatives refused to allow the citizens this right.

April 1969: At the insistence of the Milton-Park Citizens' Committee, three mini-parks were promised by Concordia for this area, and eventually created.

May 1969: There was a Milton-Park Demonstration of about 100 people at City Hall, with support from other citizens' groups. After Lucien Saulnier[1] refused to meet the representatives, a petition bearing over 800 names was delivered to him asking that the city take no action regarding urban renewal without citizen participation.

Summer 1969: Weekly film showings were held in the backyard of one of the committee members. Further negotiations with Concordia showed they pretended to discuss participation but had no intention of really allowing it.

November 1969: With the co-operation of the City of Montreal, the provincial government gave the lanes in the six-block area to Concordia. The bill of sale of the lanes from sixty years ago forbade building more than two or three storey houses, but when the lanes transferred hands, this bill of sale was annulled. This outright gift of one million dollars worth of property is a prime example of collaboration between the government and private enterprise at the expense of the citizens.

January 1970: The Committee, now incorporated, began its concentrated efforts to get signed memberships from the residents of the area. By-laws were drawn up which attempted to preserve the democratic working of the committee as well as meet with the legal standards of Quebec.

May 1970: Planning began to change the alleyways behind Basset Street and Lorne Crescent into public parks. Architects have volunteered their services to work with residents in this venture.

July 1970: The Milton-Park Street Festival. A very great community success.

CITIZEN POWER: The fundamental principle of the Milton-Park Committee is that of citizen participation in all aspects of decision-making which affect them.

The rallying point of the Milton-Park Citizens' Committee has been the protection of their area from demolition by Concordia Estates Holdings Ltd. According to the 1961 census, 71% of the houses in the area are in good condition, 25% need minor repairs, while only 4% of the houses need major repairs, Thus, 96% of the houses offered satisfactorily meet housing conditions. In spite of this data, Concordia has in the past attempted to convince the public that this area is a slum in the hope of gaining popular support for their intended project which would destroy the present community bounded by Pine Avenue on the north, Milton Street on the south, Hutchison in the west and Ste. Famille in the east. The present low rental housing would be replaced by commercial buildings (including a 29 floor office building and a hotel of 500 rooms) and a high-rise apartment complex containing a large proportion of bachelor apartments which would rent at $180 a month for a room with a kitchenette. Current rents are at $130 a month for nine room homes.

There is presently an acute shortage of low-rent housing in Montreal. "During the past six years, Montreal has witnessed the destruction of some ten thousand units of low income accommodation...Private redevelopment of the inner city of the magnitude of Cité Concordia will augment this shocking total." (The Committee on Housing and Urban Renewal of the Montreal Metropolitan Region, Nov. 1969).

Concordia itself now admits that their scheme of relocating tenants in houses vacated in the area is only short term.

"We recognize that relocation is a short-term solution. As we build we keep reducing the portion of the housing stock which we can offer at low rentals" (Herb Auerbach, September 17, 1969[2]). This is to say that people will be relocated in existing houses for only the four years that comprise Phase One of the project.

Although Concordia has spoken of an "agreement in principle" between Concordia and the Quebec Housing Corporation to provide low rent units in Cité Concordia, such an agreement is not possible under present law, and has been denied repeatedly by Quebec Housing.

Concordia is clearly finding it difficult to finance Cité Concordia. To date (Jan. 1971) they have held three unveilings; in 1968, 1969, and again in 1970. Each unveiling has been a fund-seeking affair; the change from year to year being the increasing quantity of commercial units and the corresponding decrease in residential buildings. They cannot yet be definite about when they will start demolition and construction.

"The city planning department survey shows that citizens moved from the Little Burgundy slums into the new St. Martin Blocks public housing apartments[3] now pay 83% more for rent than they did before. Planners feel that the record provides an argument in favour of providing housing to low income groups through restoration of older houses and rent subsidies paid directly to citizens instead of putting the accent on new buildings. They base their arguments not only on the higher cost—and higher rents—of new public housing, but on the effects of these higher rents on the social fabric of slum areas. As Hans Blumenfeld, a noted city planner, puts it, "The war on slums all too often appears to be a war on slum victims" (The Montreal Star).

Despite Concordia's eight year neglect of much of their property, "restoration of the area would be minimal" according to Aimé Desautels, director of the City Planning Department (May 26, 1969).

The Milton-Park Citizens' Committee has been incorporated as a non-profit association with the legal possibility of buying and administering houses on a non-profit basis for the benefit of low-income residents of the area. This alternative has been well researched and declared economically feasible by both the citizens' committee and the Quebec Housing Corporation. The citizens and the QHC are now negotiating low-interest loans for fifty-year periods in order to enable the Citizens' Corporation to buy houses in the Milton-Park area.

Following is a resumé of the different sub-committees working within the Milton-Park Citizens' Committee:

Daycare
Milton-Park is exploring a variety of possible ways in which inexpensive daycare can be provided.

Alleyways Committee
The Alleyways Committee is involved with promoting neighbourhood co-operation in attempting to change backyards and alleyways into attractive public parks where everyone can enjoy themselves. To date, the area of Basset St. is the focus of this community project. Citizen participation in the preliminary stages in both projects has been enthusiastic and the Basset St. group has already approached the city and are now at the stage of finalizing their plans.

Bulldozer
Bulldozer is a community newspaper distributed about every three weeks within the Milton-Park area since 1968. It prints ideas on housing and community co-operation. It attempts to bring to the community attention the philosophy and actions of the Milton-Park Citizens' Committee.

Publicity Committee
The Publicity Committee prepares and distributes press releases. Occasionally it holds press conferences. All statements which it intends to release must be cleared at the Tuesday night general meeting except when a Tuesday meeting authorizes the committee to act between meetings. The activity is usually restricted to newspapers, TV and radio. Other types of public are handled by the other MPCC committees. We welcome your help, surtout si vous parlez français.

The Activity Committee
This group plans and puts on festivals (such as the Summer Street Festival), benefit concerts, movie showings, etc.

Workshop Committee
This sub-committee is in the midst of creating a craft workshop for the area in which people may develop skills and eventually sell products.

Housing Committee
The sub-committee which is planning citizen-owned low-rent housing in the district and negotiating with Quebec Housing.

Medical Clinic
Milton-Park will begin a free Community Clinic at the end of January. Doctors, nurses, supplies, and space have been found, but the day-to-day work of contact with the people and running the clinic needs many volunteers.

SO IT IS TIME TO MAKE A STAND

- Various actions are possible in order to pressure those responsible for the situation.
- We can present our case against Concordia at a hearing of the Rental Control Board, who can refuse Concordia its demolition permits.
- We are working out an alternate plan for the renovation and preservation of the neighbourhood.
- We can use a rent strike to back Concordia down—we deposit our rents with a lawyer, to back up our demands.
- We can picket and demonstrate in front of Concordia's offices to publicize our situation and get public opinion on our side.
- We can join forces with citizens across the City who are fighting similar battles and who agree with us that Concordia is only one example of a vicious system that sacrifices people to profits.

CITIZEN POWER WILL STOP CONCORDIA

NOTES

1. Saulnier was Chair of the Montreal Executive Committee from 1960–1969.
2. Herb Auerbach was the project manager for Concordia Estates.
3. Îlots Saint-Martin, in Montreal's southwest neighbourhood of Little Burgundy, was built in 1969 and consists of 307 apartments for families and six apartments used as common areas. It is public housing, owned and administered by the Office municipal d'habitation de Montréal.

Communauté Milton-Parc: How We Did It and How It Works Now

Lucia Kowaluk and Carolle Piché-Burton

The First Hundred Years

The residential area of Milton-Parc and the streets surrounding it were constructed during the second half of the 19th century to serve bourgeois families. The Hôtel-Dieu Hospital, opened in 1862, was a focal point, built on a section of a huge tract of land which had been owned since the 18th century by Les Religieuses Hôpitalières de Saint-Joseph and had been founded by Jeanne Mance in the 17th century. Part of the land not used for the hospital and convent was developed for greystone row housing starting with Sainte-Famille Street, designed to lead north from Sherbrooke Street, with a view directly to the Nuns' Chapel.

The other streets from University Street to Saint Laurent Boulevard followed rapidly as the new electric tramway, which connected Old Montreal to the flat farmland of the Milton-Parc area, made transportation comfortable between new residential and old commercial areas.

Following World War II, the 75- to 100-year old housing became less desirable. Families gradually moved out, some selling to new owners, others converting the large cottages and duplexes into rooming houses. Some buildings burned, while others were torn down deliberately; in both cases new low-rise housing or larger high-rises were constructed. The neighbourhood, while still very comfortable and liveable, became shabby.

1960-1972

In the mid-1960s, when tearing down and rebuilding became the desirable form of urban renewal, a group of developers, who were close friends, slowly bought up 90% of the buildings that stood on the six-block area between Hutchison, Pine, Sainte-Famille and Milton. They offered generous prices and acted through four different numbered companies. By 1968, they owned all but the churches, two schools, and a handful of original houses. Their plan was to tear down everything but the institutions and construct a new, shiny, modern city: high-rises, offices, and commercial buildings. While the Drapeau city administration was thrilled, the residents were alarmed, and the Milton-Parc Citizens' Committee was born.

The late 1960s was not only a time of modern urban renewal; it was also a time of social change, working for social justice, wanting a "better world," and fighting back. The University Settlement on Saint Urbain near Prince Arthur, part of the late-19th century settlement movement which offered services of recreation and education to the poor, was also part of the social ferment.

While the University Settlement was founded to serve the poor, it began to change to working with the poor. The staff of social workers, community organizers, and the users of the University Settlement began to organize together to save their neighbourhood. While the overwhelming leadership of this thrust was assumed by social workers and urban planners, residents slowly and cautiously became involved, and their numbers grew.

From 1968 to 1972, people from the Citizens' Committee and the University Settlement knocked on doors; signed petitions; demonstrated in the streets; marched to City Hall; worked with McGill University architecture students to present alternatives to high-rises; held street festivals; tried to form a housing co-operative; founded alternative services such as a community health clinic, daycares, and a food-buying co-op; and held endless meetings, all the while struggling with lengthy discussions and a commitment to democratic functioning.

At the same time, the owners of the properties (now named Concordia Estates Ltd.) began working on Phase One of their project: the tenants in certain designated blocks or parts of blocks were forced to move out. In May 1972, the Milton-Parc Citizens' Committee occupied some of the empty dwellings and, simultaneously, a dozen particularly courageous individuals occupied the offices of Concordia Estates Ltd. on Parc Avenue (where the tennis courts now stand). On May 26, 1972, 59 individuals were arrested, booked at the police station, and charged with public mischief. Following the trial of eight of those individuals, the jury acquitted everyone on February 7, 1973. However, it "took the wind out of everyone's sails." People were exhausted, and they felt they had failed.

1972-1979

Meanwhile, things were not going so well for the developers. The militant activity of the Citizens' Committee had drawn the attention of some of their financial supporters. A major backer of the La Cité project, the Ford Foundation, withdrew its funding. The worldwide oil crisis of 1972 and construction activities linked to the 1976 Montreal Olympics, which caused a huge jump in inflation, had the effect of severely decreasing the value of the funding planned by Concordia Estates Ltd. for all three phases of the development. Although they proceeded with Phase One, constructing the buildings we now have among us—an office tower, three apartment high-rises, an underground shopping mall, and a hotel (which is now a McGill residence)—they could not continue and decided to divide the neighbourhood. Concordia continued to own the one third that was under construction for Phase One, while the remaining two-thirds of the old original properties came under the ownership and management of a newly-created company, Paxmil, with offices at the northeast corner of Parc and Milton. By 1974, neighbourhood activities were at a standstill.

But not for long. The excavations and construction involved in building Phase One disrupted traffic for the surrounding streets. The Jeanne-Mance Street Committee was formed with the goal of eliminating through traffic, including buses, on Jeanne-Mance.

The tried and true method of non-violent militant action went into gear, including petitions, door-to-door organizing, and sit-downs at intersections to block traffic (including a "picnic supper" at the intersection of Jeanne-Mance and Prince Arthur). The Grayson Report, a serious academic paper, presented valid and efficient alternatives for rerouting buses and traffic.

It took some years, but eventually the City's Traffic Department saw it our way. An equally important result was the active involvement of a new group of residents who joined the Milton-Parc Citizens' Committee, where many old-timers continued as well.

In 1977, the community learned, through the grapevine, that Concordia Estates Ltd. and Paxmil were interested in selling off the remaining two-thirds of their original project. Funding had dried up.

Community organizers took a fresh look at their strategy and realized a new start was in order. The Milton-Parc saga was relaunched and the timing could not have been better, as three important factors came together:

- The Parti Quebecois had formed government in Quebec and promised a referendum on sovereignty. While this was exciting and positive for many, other parts of society became very anxious, many businesses left the province, and real estate values stagnated or plummeted. There was no market for Concordia's old urban housing and the developers wanted to be relieved of it.
- The neighbourhood now had nearly ten years of experience in "militant action": working together, understanding the role of non-violent direct action, trusting each other, understanding the need for giving volunteer time, and using the principles of transparency and democratic functioning, as well as the ability to analyze how society and the economy work. Large numbers of residents wanted to form housing co-operatives.
- With the help of a grant from Heritage Montreal, and more help from a newly formed Technical Resource Group (GRT) and the CDLC (Le Conseil de Développement de Logement Communautaire), research was carried out on the possibility of buying the property, the legal requirements of forming housing co-operatives, and the existence of political will at all three levels of

government to support and finance such a project. The research showed the way: the political will was there, as was very helpful support for the project from the city-wide heritage conservation movement (Heritage Montreal and Save Montreal), and the neighbourhood was ready. On May 16, 1979, the Government of Canada, through its housing agency the Canada Mortgage and Housing Corporation (CMHC), bought the property for $5.5 million using a federal program already in place, created by the Trudeau government, to help tenants form co-operatives.

At the time, CMHC promised to sell the properties to the Société du Patrimoine Urbain de Montréal (SPUM), a newly formed non-profit corporation created with the help of Heritage Montreal. It gave SPUM full responsibility to manage the properties, and made a commitment to SPUM of its intent to provide financial support to Milton-Parc co-operatives and other non-profit associations. The first challenge for SPUM and the Milton-Parc community was to provide a viable and feasible Action Plan within six months.

To prepare the Action Plan, technical support was provided by the CDLC, assisted by the newly formed Milton-Parc Technical Resource Group.

A very well thought-out Action Plan was prepared and in April 1980, CMHC officially accepted this plan. However, CMHC indicated that future rents would be based on market levels, and there was no guarantee the rents would remain affordable, nor that residents would not be permanently displaced.

Needless to say, this was traumatic for the residents in Milton-Parc and the community was quick to mobilize again. This mobilization coincided with the coming referendum on sovereignty on May 20, 1980, and the federal government, not wanting any unnecessary disruptions, acted quickly. The neighbourhood successfully argued the new rents for the renovated dwellings were not to be based on the market, but rather on rents currently paid, with modest increases. No residents would be forced to leave their units due to financial reasons.

CMHC committed to provide substantial subsidies for the purchase and renovation of the buildings to ensure the affordable rent structure, as well as the cost of the Technical Resource Group.

A new non-profit corporation, the Société d'Amélioration Milton-Parc (SAMP), with a board composed of residents and experts in law, architecture, urban planning, business and community development, was formed to become the temporary owner of the properties. SAMP would oversee the work and eventually turn the properties over to the co-ops and other non-profits, which would then own the properties. CMHC sold the properties to SAMP in October 1980.

The GRT was made up of 20 skilled and committed people who were social animators, educators, architects, and administrators. Its purpose was to assist the community, the co-ops and non-profits to create their organizations, to provide the technical resources in relation to the renovations (prepare the plans, obtain permit approvals, prepare and manage the tendering process and supervise the quality, budgets and schedules of the works), and to manage financing and relationships with the three levels of government. The GRT also facilitated the transfer of ownership from SAMP to the individual housing co-ops and non-profit housing associations.

1980-1987

The financing of each co-op, unique to Milton-Parc, was complex. It was subject to certain regulations demanded by CMHC as a condition of receiving the funding, which included the generous subsidies which kept the rents low. As eventual owner of its own buildings, each co-op and other non-profit associations would hold a 35-year mortgage, guaranteed by CMHC, from a bank or financial institution in order to pay for its share of the renovations and purchase price. CMHC, financed by federal taxes, would subsidize the whole project. CMHC paid the difference between the interest rate at the time and a set rate of 2%. This meant that rents were calculated to finance the cost of a mortgage at only 2% plus property taxes, maintenance, insurance and utilities. The rents would be below market and would be based on the "acquired rights" of the original residents to remain in their dwellings.

During the 35-year period when CMHC would guarantee the mortgage and subsidize the project, it had certain requirements:

- The renovations had to meet certain standards of safety and health;
- The buildings had to be maintained in a constant state of good repair;
- At least 15% of the residents of each co-op and other non-profit had to be eligible for an additional subsidy, bringing their rents to no more than 30% of their very low incomes. CMHC's financing included a specific subsidy, rent-geared-to-income, to be used for this purpose;
- A certain percentage of each co-op and other non-profit budget had to go toward a reserve fund to pay for major repairs, which could only be used with CMHC's permission;
- CMHC had to be kept up to date regarding the co-ops' and other non-profits' internal functioning, with annual reports of the co-ops' and non-profits' audits, annual general assembly minutes, elected officers, and adherence to rent-geared-to-income regulations.

There were almost 600 dwelling units in 135 buildings in Milton-Parc. The total cost of development was $30.7 million. The CMHC, the City of Montreal, and the

Quebec Government contributed $6 million in capital subsidies. The remaining amount was borrowed on mortgage loans and the CMHC entered into an agreement with each co-op and other non-profit to subsidize the mortgage rate down to 2%. In the first year this amounted to $4 million. The amount varied over 35 years, tied to the changes in the interest rate upon renewal of the mortgage loans.

The first eight co-ops self-organized through affinity very quickly (1979-80). These co-ops formed from the buildings where all the community organizers were living: Du Nordet, Milton-Parc, Les Tourelles, Sainte-Famille, Concerto, Petite Cité, Du Chez Soi, and La Tour des Alentours. CMHC required that 50% plus one of the residents of the dwellings involved had to agree to form a co-op. These first eight co-ops, working closely with SAMP (which was still the owner), immediately applied for, and received, their mortgage loans. From the beginning, co-ops controlled their own finances.

The period from 1979 to 1987, when the properties were turned over to the co-ops and other non-profits, was eight years of hard work by staff and volunteers alike under the leadership of the director. This was creative and imaginative work. It involved ingenious methods of problem-solving ("There's a problem? We'll solve it!"), a lot of learning about renovations and the running of co-ops and other non-profits, and a commitment to democratic functioning.

Beginning as soon as CMHC had bought the property, the community began to meet on a fairly regular basis. In the first year, the Action Plan was prepared and presented to the community. At this very early stage two major and important questions were discussed: 1) What kind of structure would be created to govern the entirety of the community? and 2) What were the basic social values and how would they be guaranteed for all co-ops and other non-profits? In terms of structure, proposals included a "Federation of Milton-Parc Co-ops," or a "Conseil Milton-Parc." The social values included the essentials of abolishing speculation on any resale of property and preserving the socio-economic demographics of the community which was primarily low-income.

The Action Plan prepared by SPUM and the community in 1979–80 provided the following ten principles:

1. No original resident would be forced out for economic reasons;
2. The properties would be owned and administered on a non-profit basis;
3. Ultimate control of the community would be in the hands of the residents;
4. Small groups would be formed to own and administer the properties;
5. No original resident would be forced out because they do not wish to be involved in the administration of the property in which they reside;
6. The buildings would be renovated;
7. Government funding from all levels would be used;

8. The resources and skills needed to provide the goals of the project would be provided;
9. Resources which existed in the project and in the surrounding community would be used;
10. To meet the financial goals as well as the goal of resident control, all the properties would be transferred by May 1982.

All these goals and principles were respected. The only exception was the date of transfer, which was pushed to 1987 in order to allow time for community discussion on the legal form the transfer would take, the organization and incorporation of all co-ops and other non-profits, and the completion of the renovations.

There was strong agreement within the community on these ten principles, as expressed in minutes and documents that were distributed widely. Additional principles declared right from the beginning were:

- Buildings already subdivided into rooming houses or tiny apartments would remain that way, since they provided much-needed housing for single, low-income residents;
- The heritage features of the buildings would be preserved and maintained;
- Buildings already used as residences could not be transformed into commercial premises.

By 1984, seven more co-ops were organized with the help of the Milton-Parc Technical Resource Group: Rue des Artistes, Les Jardins, Petite Hutchison, L'Alliance, L'Escale, Les Colonnes, and La Voie Lactée. Three non-profits, Porte Jaune, 55-65, and Chambrelle, were formed from buildings that housed individuals in rooms or tiny apartments, most of whom were people who were not interested in or able to manage their buildings without outside help. A fourth non-profit, Chambreclerc, was set up in 1989, built on two pieces of vacant land within the project to house previously homeless individuals.

A separate non-profit corporation, Société de Développement Communautaire Milton-Parc (SDC), was formed to manage the commercial properties on Parc Ave., Milton, and Prince Arthur.

In addition, two more non-profits, Société Village Jeanne-Mance and Societé Allegro, were formed by the individuals who had previously hoped to buy their property as private owners, the story of which is described below.

Before the Communauté Milton-Parc

We need to go back a few years. The first idea of ownership was that each co-op and non-profit would become the sole owner of its buildings and land. However, once the property had been turned over to SPUM, about a dozen individuals, among the 1,000 or more residents then residing in Milton-Parc, declared their interest in owning, as individuals, the property they lived in. Their interest was not an unusual one in our society, in which the norm is exactly that: residents own their property if they can afford it. However, most of the residents involved in the project did not agree. There were a number of reasons why:

- The ten-year struggle to save the neighbourhood had been governed by the principle that everyone already there—most of whom, according to surveys taken at the time, had very low incomes—could stay in their homes at rents they could afford;
- The community activists had not given thousands of volunteer hours over ten years so that a handful of individuals could buy property at a very low price and then reap the benefits of a huge increase in property values which would inevitably happen in the next few years. According to these activists, the property had not been saved for speculation;
- As one resident said, "They want the price of one steak at the same rate as the whole cow." According to one calculation, the $6 million total purchase cost, divided by a little over 600 units, would come to an average of $10,000 per unit! Obviously this huge advantage for a dozen or so residents was out of the question;
- SPUM, the GRT, and a large consensus in the community agreed that the properties should be owned on a non-profit basis. This was enshrined in the Action Plan in 1979 and was the basis on which CMHC subsequently agreed to make its programs available when it approved the Action Plan in 1980.

Although this small group of self-interested residents was defeated, a number of them were not interested in forming housing co-ops. With their ambition for private ownership unrealizable, they elected instead to create non-profit housing associations, and Société Village Jeanne-Mance and Société Allegro were born.

Three big questions remained about the future of the neighbourhood: 1) How would the properties be protected from market pressures to increase value in a choice location in downtown Montreal? 2) How would the project's affordability be ensured to protect low-income people, when they are often pushed out as a neighbourhood is improved? 3) How would the heritage qualities of the buildings be preserved?

Searching for Answers to These Questions

The community's restrictions on affordability and architectural preservation were unprecedented. At that time, CMHC's equity requirements for its co-operative projects were much less restrictive than what the community wanted and there were no provincial or municipal heritage restrictions for Milton-Parc. But the residents agreed these restrictions were essential in order to preserve the unique social and historic features of the neighbourhood. No simple legal framework to permit these requirements appeared possible.

The first proposal came after CMHC transferred ownership to SAMP. SAMP decided it would sign 99-year leases with the co-ops and non-profit housing groups. These leaseholder agreements would contain provisions regarding architectural preservation and new unit allocation.

The response from many of the residents who had worked the hardest to organize the co-ops was strong opposition. They wanted their groups to be full-fledged owners, not some sort of tenant. SAMP said this was impossible but some residents sought advice from other legal experts. After long discussion in the community and with SAMP, it was realized that if the legal structure did not permit such mechanisms, the legal structure would have to be amended.

The Creation of the Communauté Milton-Parc

One of Quebec's most eminent notaries and a scholar in the matter, François Frenette, was recruited to assist in legally structuring the Milton-Parc housing project. He proposed the idea of a condominium in which each co-op and non-profit would own their buildings and the land under the buildings. The land adjacent to the buildings (both in the front and the back) would be held as common property by all the co-op and other non-profit owners in Milton-Parc. Only the occupants who live in the buildings could use those adjacent pieces of land. Frenette suggested a creative solution whereby the entire ensemble of buildings would be owned by the co-ops and non-profits without dividing them into individual units, as is done in condominiums comprising separate dwellings. A draft "Declaration of Co-ownership" (the Declaration), was formally presented to the community on May 20, 1986.

The Declaration, however, goes further than the commercial condominiums familiar to our society. Just as individuals purchasing a unit in a newly built condominium project must agree to certain rules such as the number of pets or a prohibition on changing the windows in their apartment, the co-owners—co-ops and other non-profit groups of Milton-Parc—would enter into a co-propriety agreement in which they would agree to allocate a large portion of newly available dwellings to very-low and low-income households and would agree to maintain the architectural heritage qualities of their façades.

The community continued to meet frequently, even weekly, throughout 1986 and 1987, and several refinements were made to the social and economic values:

- Residents already living in the buildings before renovations would have acquired rights;
- Income and space requirements would apply only during the selection process for new members;
- The acquired rights would apply to residents in perpetuity, meaning residents would not be forced to downsize or leave if their income and family size changed.

On June 12, 1987 all the co-ops and other non-profits signed an agreement to accept the Declaration as the fundamental legal document describing their ownership rights and responsibilities. The signatories included the group that had previously wanted to have individual ownership. The final agreement included provisions that met their concerns, namely that the organization would concern itself exclusively with the administration of the properties. It would not take positions on political or social issues affecting the community, without the consent of the whole community. This agreement was drafted into a private bill and presented to the Quebec National Assembly. It was adopted on June 23, 1987 and the Declaration became law.

The Declaration describes the governing structure of the "condominium for social purposes"—the Communauté Milton-Parc (CMP). In legal terms, the CMP is a "syndicate." Each co-op and non-profit owns their buildings and the land directly underneath their buildings while CMP owns the common land, such as the alleyways and the yards. CMP became the governing body for the entire neighbourhood, comprised of representatives from each co-op and non-profit. Its collective responsibility is to preserve the properties, ensure the principles of the Declaration are honoured by all co-ops and non-profits, maintain and manage the common portions, protect property rights of the community, and take all measures in the common interest.

The Declaration spells out the legally binding conditions to which the CMP, co-ops and other non-profits must adhere:

- Milton-Parc exists to allow low- and moderate-income people access to quality housing;
- The urban fabric and the architectural and socio-economic uniqueness of the neighbourhood must be conserved;
- Speculation is prevented through the application of stringent mechanisms.

These conditions are found in the Declaration's "Destination Clause," which can only be altered with a "unanimous vote of all the co-owners." In other words, a majority of 100% of the co-owners would need to be achieved amongst all the co-ops and non-profits to make any change to the guiding principles of the CMP.

When the Québec Civil Code came into force in 1994, the rules regarding voting in a co-ownership syndicate changed. However, unanimous consent of all co-owners to make changes directly or indirectly to the Destination Clause is still required for the CMP, since its Declaration had been drawn up before 1994.

What has made the CMP unique is that it attaches social responsibility and non-speculative restraints on the collective ownership of the property. This is similar to the way any restrictions can be established in a land trust, a legal status that is accepted and used elsewhere in North America.

In December 1987, when renovations were finished, the co-ops and non-profits had all been formed, financing was in order, and the Declaration was completed, SAMP and each co-op and non-profit signed the deed of sale. It was a great day—a new chapter for Milton-Parc had just begun.

The CMP is unique in all of North America. It is the only land trust in which co-ops or non-profits are governed by a declaration of co-ownership. It is also unique in its conception: it is the result of a 20-year struggle undertaken by tenants to save their neighbourhood. It is a legacy that must be preserved.

1988-2018: CMP Controls Its Neighbourhood

The fourth phase of Milton-Parc had now begun. Over the past 30 years, the residents have had to manage their affairs, become landlords of very valuable property as well as members and tenants of a co-op or non-profit, work together to manage the land owned in common, and handle the social problems that arise when any group of people has to collectively manage their living environment.

Soon after the private bill was adopted, the CMP rented an office, hired a manager to take care of the administration, and established a democratic decision-making structure. A board of directors was elected and began holding general assemblies, consisting of one delegate from each of its member organizations: 15 housing co-ops, six non-profit housing corporations, and the SDC (which manages the commercial properties).

The general assemblies function according to the arrangements described in the Declaration. Each co-owner manages its own internal operations and abides by the conditions and restraints described in the Declaration, while the CMP manages common concerns such as property evaluations, insurance, and land not managed by a co-op or non-profit. It can also propose arbitration in the case of conflict between co-owners or between the CMP and co-owners.

The CMP administrators are obliged to ensure the Declaration is followed and the Destination Clause is respected.

Municipal property taxes and school taxes are sent to the CMP in one large invoice for the common spaces. These are paid by the member groups according to an ingenious system based on the amount of land each member co-op and other non-profit manages. The result—which is very fair—is that groups with large pieces of land around their buildings, like Co-op Milton-Parc, Co-op Concerto, or Société d'Habitation Chambrelle, pay a much higher share of the taxes, insurances, and fees. Co-ops and non-profits with very little land, like Co-op Les Jardins and Société d'Habitation Chambreclerc, pay a very low share of these shared costs. A proportional representation plan prescribed by the Declaration is also used in weighting the votes during the general assemblies.

Regarding city property taxes, in 1987, SAMP challenged the City's assessment of the value of the Milton-Parc properties, which were about to be transferred to the co-owners. In a decision dated August 27, 1987, the Bureau de Révision de l'Évaluation Foncière du Québec ruled the evaluation of the properties for tax purposes should be based on their decreased non-market value because of the rules preventing resale for non-speculative purposes. This was an ideal outcome, as it was in line with the Declaration.

The CMP has been built on a solid foundation, going back to the struggle which began in 1968. It has become a wonderful and sustained alternative to the capitalist housing market. It has upheld the values of its residents to control their community, manage their homes collectively, and function democratically.

For a more complete document on the Milton-Parc Project including the social contract (the Declaration) that binds the CMP together, the entire document and other material is available online at http://www.miltonparc.org/

October 17, 1969
Free Press

Who are the friends of Milton-Park?

Not Big Businessmen

The Concordia bosses would probably like to be thought of as progressive, liberal-minded men. But the facts of economic control speak differently. The Ford Foundation is a major contributor to the exploitation of black people in American ghettos, and to strategic research that helps the United States enslave the nations of Asia and Africa to its own economic interests. Never has a "charitable" institution been founded on such all-consuming greed. Great West Life is linked by directorships to companies that involve themselves in gassing workers through negligence (INCO), manufacturing chemical weapons for the American war machine (Canadian Industries Limited or CIL), and maintaining the economic power of the ruling white minority in South Africa (Rothman's). Can the men who control companies such as these be expected to put the needs and desires of ordinary citizens above their own profits?

Not Politicians

Not only do Concordia's financial "friendships" explain their attitudes toward citizens, they also say a lot about the postures of politicians. Concordia president Gauvreau, both as a prominent civil engineer and as chairman of the MTC [Montreal Transportation Commission], is probably on excellent terms with City Hall. This, and Concordia's prior involvement in Place Bonaventure, may explain the Drapeau-Saulnier administration's "hands off" position. Concordia also benefits from a strange coincidence whereby members of the Richardson family sit on both the Great West Board of Directors and on the Trudeau cabinet. Furthermore, the influence of media czar Paul Desmarais and of such conglomerates of economic power as the Bank of Montreal-CPR group on all three levels of government cannot be underestimated.

Not the Universities

Members of the McGill Board of Governors are big businessmen who have intimate tie-ins with the conglomerates of capital that control Concordia. The Université de Montréal has received grants from the Ford Foundation to do social research for Concordia.

All the power to the people!
Against the formidable power of organized finance, only the power of organized citizens—the power of ordinary people fighting for social justice—has any chance of winning.

Concordia's friends

James Richardson & Sons
A family of Winnipeg grain magnates, the head of which is now a minister in Trudeau's cabinet.

Power Corporation
A $3 billion conglomerate, Power Corporation is 51% owned by a combination of Paul Desmarais' Gelco Enterprises and the Peter Thomson interests. It is linked to major finance companies such as Laurentide Financial Corp. and Union Acceptance Corp. Desmarais, its chief executive officer and chairman, owns four Quebec daily newspapers (including La Presse), a chain of weeklies and several radio and TV stations.

Ford Foundation
Along with Great West Life, the Ford Foundation is one of Concordia's major backers. Founded in the 1930's as a means of evading inheritance and wealth taxes, the Foundation is the largest "charitable" organization in the world. Some of its "charitable" ventures have included giving the RAND corporation (an American war research outfit) its start and buying off militant black leaders who were a threat to white big business in U.S. cities. Ford's support of Concordia is an investment and not "charity." But it did make a "charitable" donation to a Université de Montréal group for special research in the Milton-Park area that greatly benefitted Concordia. (N.B. Unconfirmed reports earlier had it that Ford had withdrawn its backing of Concordia for fear of bad publicity. It is likely, however, that at least part of the investment remains intact).

Royal Bank of Canada
Canadian Imperial Bank of Commerce
Investors Group

The most influential financial company in Canada. Investors Group brings together money from five major sources (as shown here) which represent all the important concentrations of capital in Canada.

Imperial Life Assurance Co.
This Toronto-based firm has the biggest share (30%) in Investors Group. It is 51% owned by Power Corp.

Canadian Pacific Investments Ltd.
Part of the massive Canadian Pacific Railway-Bank of Montreal empire.

Great West Life Assurance
A major investor in the Concordia project. Directors of this Winnipeg-based firm also sit on the boards of such financial giants as the International Nickel Company, the Bank of Montreal, Canadian Industries Limited, all the big western grain corporations, and the South African-based tobacco concern Rothman's of Pall Mall Canada Ltd. Great West is 51% owned by the Investors Group.

Concordia Estates Holdings Ltd.
This is the company at the centre of the Concordia group. The President, Brigadier J.G. Gauvreau, is a former civil engineer. He's also Chairman and General Manager of the Montreal Transportation Commission (MTC) and Vice-President of Dow Brewery Ltd.

Concordia Estates Ltd.
Responsible for planning and development of the Cité Concordia project. Big wheels in this company are A. Isseman (Chairman) and N. Nerenberg (President) (both former). Other projects have included the posh Place Bonaventure development.
Concordia Management Services Ltd.
Concordia Construction Inc.
Concordia Realties Ltd.

Champlain Housing Trust

Brenda Torpy

The Champlain Housing Trust (CHT), founded in Burlington, Vermont, in 1984, was born in a small city with a big idea: by creating a stock of permanently affordable housing, everyone could have access to a decent home, regardless of income. This was the grand vision of a newly elected progressive government, led by Mayor Bernie Sanders, who came into office in 1981, the same year that Ronald Reagan began his own two-term presidency.

The Reagan Revolution forced the Sanders' administration to develop innovative solutions for the housing problems in Burlington, Vermont within the context of the federal withdrawal of needed funding from affordable housing and community development programs. Equally challenging were double-digit mortgage rates that prevailed during the early 1980s, the threatened gentrification of Burlington's traditional working class neighbourhoods, and the long-standing neglect of housing quality and affordability issues by previous mayors, who had favored downtown commercial development and bulldozed low-income neighbourhoods in the name of urban renewal.

A cornerstone of the progressive agenda was to open up city hall to all citizens—especially those who had been previously excluded in decisions about city planning and public funding. The community land trust (CLT) model discovered by a Progressive Party alderman named Terry Bouricius looked like a good fit. The model's democratic structure and its commitment to permanent affordability made a lot of sense in a city where housing costs seemed to rise in every economic cycle; where a lack of code enforcement and the absence of landlord-tenant law made low-income tenants nearly powerless in the overheated housing market; and where proposed waterfront development adjacent to the city's lowest-income area, the Old North End, threatened further gentrification.

When Mayor Sanders created the Community and Economic Development Office (CEDO) in 1982 to help implement his progressive agenda, work on establishing a community land trust soon got underway. CEDO sent three employees to the first national CLT gathering in Voluntown, Connecticut, hosted by the Institute for Community Economics (ICE). Included in this CEDO delegation were Michael Monte, the City's community development director, and myself, as I was the City's housing director at the time. At the Voluntown conference, we met John Davis, who was a technical assistance provider on ICE's staff. A few months later, CEDO contracted with ICE to bring Davis to Burlington in order to introduce the CLT idea to Burlington's citizens and to see if it would take root.

CEDO saw its primary role as engaging citizens to address their own needs and problems and then supporting them with funding and technical assistance. The CLT effort followed this model. As people heard about this new approach to affordable housing, they very quickly embraced it. Stakeholders included tenant rights activists and neighbourhood leaders, affordable housing experts, and other advocates for social and economic justice.

The Burlington Community Land Trust (BCLT) was incorporated in 1984 after thousands of hours of volunteer work. Recruited and coordinated by CEDO staff, these volunteers formed by-laws, developed policies, and fashioned strategies for funding the organization and for producing housing. Among the BCLT's incorporators was Howard Dean, the state's future Governor, and Sarah Carpenter, the future director of the Vermont Housing Finance Agency (VHFA). The Old North End was chosen as the BCLT's first designated Target Area.

In addition to the assistance received from both CEDO staff and Davis, the ICE staffer assigned to Burlington under a CEDO contract, the City supported the fledgling CLT effort with a $200,000 seed grant for operations, a pair of million-dollar loans from the Burlington Employee Retirement Fund, and a negotiated loan-pool from a local bank. The BCLT later received regular municipal funding for its operations and projects through federal funds that passed through the city's hands, including monies provided by the federal Community Development Block Grant and HOME programs and from local funds disbursed by Burlington's Housing Trust Fund.

The BCLT was the first municipally supported CLT in the United States, a direct result of the City of Burlington's general embrace of permanent affordability as the only socially equitable and fiscally prudent way for the public to create and sustain affordable housing. Bernie Sanders and his immediate successor, Mayor Peter Clavelle, were outspoken champions of decommodified housing. Both administrations acted to codify this principle into municipal policy and municipal ordinances. Their goal was to ensure that any public investments in affordable housing would go primarily—even exclusively—into housing that would be kept permanently affordable. At the time, this was viewed as a revolutionary idea befitting Bernie's socialist agenda, but over time, and for very practical reasons, this has become the accepted wisdom in Vermont.

None of several fledgling community land trusts that CEDO staff had learned of at Voluntown were supported by local government, and without this support they faced considerable challenges to growth and sustainability. So it was by looking northward at a slightly different model that the CEDO team saw its first incarnation of successful community land ownership at scale, that of Montreal's Milton-Parc. In 1984, Michael Monte and myself went to Montreal to visit and were deeply inspired by the leaders of the Milton-Parc Co-op and the sight of an entire City neighbourhood preserved for, and led by, its residents, including low and very low income tenants. Milton-Parc exemplified the dream that BCLT leaders had for the Old North End and over the years has provided inspiration to them. The structure of Milton-Parc also fueled the BCLT leaders' belief that limited equity co-operatives had a big role to play in the city's delivery of affordable housing and in their own neighbourhood strategy.

Thus, as Burlington's progressive leaders worked to create new resources for the development of affordable housing, they also worked to ensure the lasting affordability of any housing produced with those resources and engaged citizens in campaigns to enact new laws that would protect vulnerable renters and produce permanently affordable homes through funding and policy initiatives. This dual commitment to expanding the supply of housing and to preserving the affordability of that housing was woven into the Housing Trust Fund, capitalized through a penny increase on the property tax rate; the Inclusionary Zoning ordinance, where the affordability of all IZ units had to be preserved for 99 years; and ordinances to protect renters by regulating the conversion of rental housing to condominiums and mitigating the loss of existing housing because of demolition or conversion for commercial uses.

Creating these laws required the active participation of many of the same neighbourhood activists and housing advocates who had come together to create the BCLT in 1984. The board and staff of the BCLT were actively involved in all of these legislative efforts to expand funding for affordable housing, as well as several unsuccessful campaigns to enact ordinances to protect the rights of vulnerable renters, including an anti-speculation tax and just cause eviction rules.

There continued to be considerable overlap between city governments, the emerging Progressive Party rooted in the activists who had helped to elect Bernie Sanders, and the BCLT during the latter's early years. The BCLT's first executive director was Tim McKenzie, a neighbourhood activist who had helped to mobilize voter support for Bernie's first successful campaigns for mayor. Gretchen Bailey, an assistant city attorney who had been one of Bernie's first hires, conducted much of the legal research that enabled the BCLT to craft a ground lease compatible with Vermont law. I was the first board president of the BCLT, where I continued to serve as the city's Housing Director before moving briefly into a job at the VHFA. I was succeeded in the Housing Director's job by John Davis, the ICE employee who had assisted CEDO in establishing the BCLT, and I returned to the local scene to become the BCLT's second director in 1991.

Although Burlington was the fulcrum and the leader of the effort in Vermont to make permanent affordability the cornerstone of all housing policy, overheated market conditions throughout the state and a friendly administration in Montpelier, led by Governor Madeleine Kunin, helped the state's housing advocates bring the CLT model and other progressive solutions to the attention of the Vermont legislature and helped make permanent affordability a priority in an increasing number of state laws and plans. Vermont began experiencing a wave of speculative development in the 1980s that threatened its traditional agricultural landscape. Conservationists and housing advocates found themselves united in their opposition to the threat of unfettered land speculation, luxury development, and gentrification. Vermont was also one of the states hit the hardest by the loss of federally subsidized, privately owned rental housing as the affordability restrictions expired on these projects.

One powerful outcome of this convergence of issues was the creation of the Vermont Housing and Conservation Board (VHCB), funded by a portion of Vermont's property transfer tax to preserve open space, farms, historic landmarks, and affordable housing. The priority recipients of the grants disbursed by VHCB were to be a network of non-profits doing land conservation or affordable housing that would be called upon to steward these land-based resources permanently. VHCB helped to create and sustain the operations and projects of community land trusts not only in Burlington but throughout the state. Indeed, this new crop of CLTs became the principal means by which VHCB sought to accomplish its affordable housing mission.

The BCLT was able to grow and to thrive in this policy environment where government embraced the principle of permanent affordability and directed capital toward sustaining the residential projects and non-profit organizations that turned that social principle into the sticks and bricks of new housing. The BCLT has also benefited, along with other CLTs in Vermont, from the unusual degree of co-operation that exists in Vermont among housers, conservationists, and preservationists. Such solidarity has helped to ensure ongoing funding for VHCB, a primary source of capital for the housing developed by the BCLT and by the state's other CLTs.

As its broad policy agenda attests, the City of Burlington did not put all of its eggs in the BCLT basket, but lent its support and provided leadership to the creation of three other specialized housing non-profits covering a wide range of housing needs. These were the Committee on Temporary Shelter (COTS) to shelter the homeless; the Lake Champlain Housing Development Corporation (LCHDC), a consortium of local governments dedicated to affordable rental housing in the largely suburban metro area of Burlington; and the Champlain Valley Mutual Housing Federation (CVMHF) created to extend co-operative housing opportunities to those who could not access conventional ownership even with shared equity. The LCHDC, the CVMHF and the BCLT would all engage in bringing the co-operative housing model to the fore in the greater Burlington area. Both the Federation and the LCHDC later merged into the BCLT to form today's Champlain Housing Trust.

Housing Co-operatives—The Vermont Experience

From its earliest days the BCLT strategically purchased multi-family properties in the Old North End to avert tenant displacement. The initial vision was to work with the residents to convert these properties into small, limited equity co-operatives. But the BCLT did not take the lead in creating this new ownership opportunity for its residents. As the BCLT focused on their anti-gentrification acquisition strategy and on shared equity homeownership, CEDO laid the groundwork for the development of limited equity co-operatives and actively engaged with others in developing state-enabling legislation for co-operative housing, which passed in 1987.

In addition to CEDO, a few individuals moved this effort forward and key among them was Erhard Mahnke—a Burlington resident who served on the City Council as an independent allied with Bernie Sanders—who worked in neighbouring Winooski as the Community Development Director. On the council, Erhard was a strong supporter of the city's progressive housing agenda, and in his professional capacity in Winooski he strengthened what was a natural bond between these two cities that had so much in common in the areas of housing: historic working class neighbourhoods that were now among the state's lowest-income census tracts with very old and deteriorating housing stock; high density; and the highest ratios of renters to homeowners in Vermont.

Winooski and Burlington worked most closely through the LCHDC consortium, which also included on its board representatives of suburban communities more typical of the region around Burlington: Colchester, South Burlington and Shelburne. These suburbs had very little rental housing, let alone any affordable housing. It was a goal of both Burlington and Winooski to positively engage these suburbs in the affordable housing mission through participation in the LCHDC. The first program offered through this non-profit vehicle was discounted rehabilitation loans and services to private landlords in return for rent affordability controls. But when the 1987 tax reform created a new tax-incentive rental production program (Low Income Housing Tax credits), the LCHDC was poised to be a regional producer of new affordable rentals. It was staffed with former Winooski Public Housing Authority Director Kenn Sassorossi at the helm, with Amy Wright, CEDO's Housing Project Developer, moving over to lead project development.

In 1986 Amy Wright and Erhard Mahnke attended a conference on housing co-operatives at the University of Wisconsin in Madison. Both Madison and Milwaukee had mutual housing federations that acquired and rehabilitated small rental properties and converted them to co-ops joined together within their respective federations. This was a good model for the BCLT's burgeoning multi-family portfolio in the Old North End and for Winooski's working class neighbourhoods, and was enthusiastically embraced by the BCLT's board and staff. In 1989, the BCLT, Burlington and Winooski entered a three-party agreement to create co-ops and hired legal counsel to draft model documents as well as an organizer, John Colborn, to lead a public outreach campaign and to train Vermonters on the model. Colborn had headed the National Association of Students for Co-operation (NASCO) and became the founding director of the CVMHF when it incorporated in 1990.

The first co-ops in the Federation were conversions of small rental properties in Burlington's Old North End and in Winooski. The LCHDC developed and built the first new construction co-ops: Flynn Avenue with 28 homes and Thelma Maple co-op with 20. Flynn was the first and last co-op financed with a blanket mortgage and the only shared equity co-op. In order to meet the affordability missions of all three non-profits, subsequent co-ops were funded with the same federal subsidies and tax-incentivized investments as their rental developments. Projects funded with these needed to be structured as individual limited partnerships. In this hybrid model the co-op corporation derived its rights of ownership and control through a master-lease from the partnership to the co-op. This created zero equity co-ops accessible to very low income people. The cost of the share equals one month's rent that also acts as the security deposit.

The BCLT converted an old bakery into the Rose Street Artists' co-op with 12 live-work spaces and a large interior gallery in the Target Area. It also created a downtown co-op of 31 homes called Park Place in a historic former hotel that had become a tenement building. In South Burlington, the BCLT and the LCHDC partnered to create a small neighbourhood with an 18 home co-op and five shared equity homes. The Mutual Housing Federation provided training and technical assistance to each of the co-ops, and was governed by a board with a super majority of co-op residents and a minority of community representatives including the BCLT and CEDO. The federation also secured a master loan agreement with a local bank to provide financing to the co-ops.

As the 1990s progressed and federal cutbacks deepened, the City of Burlington, the main source of capacity funding, struggled to maintain its non-profit housing network. The Co-op Federation had the biggest challenge because it was very grant-dependent. The co-op member fees made up a small fraction of the costs of operation and the work, with so many small co-ops, was very labour intensive. The BCLT's membership fees were also still modest but, like the LCHDC, they earned fees for developing and managing their properties. In 1996 the board of the Co-op Federation commissioned a sustainability report and decided that the co-ops would be more stable as part of a larger entity. They chose the BCLT because it was also a membership organization with residents on their board. The BCLT amended their by-laws to designate one seat and a board committee for co-op residents.

Over the balance of the decade and into the next, the BCLT worked with each co-op on its needs. In the end, all but one of their small Old North End and all of the Winooski co-ops reverted back to rental. Only one large co-op opted to become rental and that was Park Place. Their decision had more to do with the interpersonal challenges among residents that had rendered the co-op inoperable. The BCLT's initial vision of converting all rentals to co-ops turned out to have been overambitious. Only a few of their acquisitions' residents had opted for the co-op model in the first place. Most chose to remain renters once their buildings were acquired by the BCLT, on which they could count for affordable rent, security of tenure and building maintenance. As a result, the BCLT had to adjust to the reality that they would become a social landlord with a major property management operation, which today makes up a large part of the CHT's operations. Currently, the surviving co-operatives are the larger ones, and the CHT provides required training and technical assistance to their boards and members.

For over a decade, the BCLT focused on improving the condition and services to this evolving portfolio of co-ops, and in 2015 was proud to develop Bright Street, its first new co-op in years as well as its largest at 40 homes. This new construction co-op in the heart of the Old North End is thriving. Multiple languages are spoken and translated at each board meeting, community gardens are shared with neighbours, and vacancies are easy to fill with committed co-operators.

Demand for co-operative living has greatly increased, and with the lessons learned from the early experiments, the CHT is poised to build on the success of Bright Street.

* * * * * *

While the Co-op Federation was being developed, the BCLT was most focused on its founding real estate strategy, which was twofold: to expand homeownership by creating a resale-restricted, leased-land homeownership product/program that would be accepted by public funders, private lenders, and prospective home buyers; and to improve the Old North End. This was a neighbourhood with an aging housing stock that despite being in poor condition was losing its affordability for the city's lower income citizens due to its proximity to the downtown, the waterfront, and the University of Vermont.

On the homeownership side, the first challenge was to gain acceptance for the CLT model and, in particular, its separation of land and improvements. This dual-ownership model scared lenders and daunted appraisers. Additionally there were few other CLTs to point to in the early 1980s and thus there was no track record to reassure skeptical lenders and public leaders that, first, there would be a market for limited equity homes on leased land, and, second, that the benefits would outweigh the risks to either buyers or lenders. Even Bernie Sanders worried that this might be "second class homeownership for working people."

The BCLT also faced the wrath of private realtors and for-profit developers who objected strenuously to the removal of land and housing from the speculative market. Some of them organized Homeowners Against the Land Trust (HALT) to oppose a proposed BCLT development in which single-family detached houses were to be built on donated land. They picketed City Hall, singing "Oh give me a home with land that I own," set to the tune of *Home On the Range*.

It was a stark reminder that what the BCLT was committed to doing was a scary departure from business as usual. Burlington's progressive government may have embraced permanent affordability as a necessary response to the inequities of a profit-oriented housing market and as a way to retain the value of the public investment in housing, but that didn't mean that the private sector—or the NIMBYs surrounding BCLT housing—were ready to do so.

The BCLT looked to the Vermont Housing Finance Agency (VHFA) for help, appealing to their public mission and offering a new tool at a time of double-digit mortgage rates. After much hemming and hawing, the VHFA accepted the CLT model, but only half-way. Their solution to getting their participating banks to chance this new thing was to create a rider to the ground lease that gave the bank the option to take the entire property (land and home) if the BCLT did not cure a default in a specified time. Confident that they would prevail and never let a property go, the BCLT reluctantly agreed to this bargain until the model was proven, at which time a more favorable lease instrument would be adopted that protected the CHT's interest in the entire property. Once the VHFA was on board, the BCLT was able to engage with local bankers who did, in time, become ardent supporters of the community land trust—especially when they realized there were virtually no foreclosures among the low-income homeowners being served by the BCLT.

The first home purchased by the BCLT was a vacant, single-family house. It had been spotted by a single mother, an assistant librarian named Kathy Neilson, who had happened to attend a public forum at the library introducing the BCLT.

Kathy wanted a decent and secure home in which to raise her two daughters and volunteered to be the "guinea pig" for the new model of tenure that the BCLT was trying to establish.

As the BCLT's founders continued to worry their way through all the structures and policies for the new CLT and continued to negotiate with the VHFA to create a mortgage product for resale-restricted homes on leased land, Kathy and her daughters cleaned up the site of what she hoped would be her new home. By autumn, she told the new BCLT board: "I mowed the grass all summer, and I'm raking the leaves now, but I will not plow the snow unless I am living there."

Goaded by this passionate, prospective homebuyer who was growing a bit impatient with how long it was taking to put a roof over her head, the BCLT's leaders speeded up their efforts to get this deal done. All the pieces were pulled together and the BCLT had its first closing in 1985. Kathy Neilson got her home at last.

The VHFA went on to create a favourable product for CLTs. It has since underwritten over $80 million in mortgages for BCLT/CHT homes. The VHFA's support introduced the model to all of the banks that use their funds and integrated the CLT mortgage into local lending. To date, 41 different lenders have made mortgages to BCLT/CHT homebuyers. The organization now has a portfolio of 603 owner-occupied houses and condominiums—in addition to approximately 2,350 homes that are owned and managed as rental or co-operative housing.

Another boost to the BCLT's homeownership program came in 1997, when the BCLT joined the NeighborWorks Network. This allowed the BCLT to access resources of the National Homeownership Campaign for the CLT's homebuyers. At that time, NeighborWorks was not known for its support of shared equity homeownership. The BCLT was one of the voices that helped to change their position by demonstrating that a homeownership model like the BCLT's could be successful, productive, and highly sustainable. Pending funding, NeighborWorks is poised to launch a national CLT shared equity homeownership program next year—the result of a long cultivation and political leadership from Vermont.

On the neighbourhood development side of its mission, the BCLT quickly evolved beyond its initial anti-gentrification commitment to the Old North End. By the 1990s, the BCLT possessed a growing portfolio of rental housing and had already started to build its internal capacity to be a good social landlord. At first it managed a relatively small number of scattered-site, rehabilitated rental properties, primarily in the Target Area. It also gradually assumed the broader community development role in the neighbourhood. Throughout the decade, the BCLT redeveloped polluted sites and returned abandoned and blighted properties to community use, including residential properties, a pocket park, a food shelf, a multi-generational community center, and buildings for non-profit offices delivering everything from affordable health care to legal services and recycled bicycles.

Also in this decade, the BCLT expanded its service area beyond the City of Burlington area to encompass all of Chittenden County and, later, all three northwest counties of Vermont, bordering Lake Champlain on the west and Canada to the north. At the request of local governments, they also began to develop new construction rentals and operate a regional rehab loan program for low-income homeowners.

The BCLT's greatest change and biggest leap came in 2005, when the leaders of the LCHDC invited the staff and board of the BCLT to explore a more formal alliance and, possibly, a merger. By that time, decades of HUD cutbacks and a draconian shredding of the social safety net by a succession of federal administrations were putting both non-profits at risk. It was no longer feasible for the LCHDC and the BCLT to share a relatively small service area of 200,000 people and to compete for a scarce supply of dollars, sites, and political support. The LCHDC possessed a large rental portfolio of 1,200 apartments. The BCLT had a portfolio of 700 homes, divided equally between rental and ownership. Neither was large enough to be truly sustainable.

After nearly a year of conversation, negotiation, and planning, the two organizations decided to merge into one. The BCLT was chosen to be the surviving corporation due to its strong membership base, broad donor support, and diversity of programs and funding sources, including those resources available through the BCLT's membership in NeighborWorks. The name chosen for the newly merged corporation was the Champlain Housing Trust, and the BCLT's executive director was selected to be the CEO.

The model of membership and governance of a "classic" CLT was embraced by both boards during the negotiations leading up to the merger, but that structure was modified slightly to incorporate the LCHDC's strong link to the municipal governments that had come together to create the LCHDC back in 1984. The CHT has continued to be structured as a membership organization with a tripartite board. A third of the governing board's directors are homeowners, renters, or co-op members who live in one of the 2,950 homes in the CHT's portfolio. Another third of the board is made up of representatives of the CHT's general membership: people who live within the CHT's service area and support the CHT's mission, but who do not live in a CHT home. The final third of the board is made up of officials from the public sector, drawn from various municipal governments and regional bodies within the CHT's three-county service area.

The production, management, maintenance, and stewardship of the CHT's ever-expanding portfolio of permanently affordable housing currently occupies a staff of 90 employees, headquartered in Burlington. This portfolio serves the

CHT's vision of providing a diverse continuum of housing options for low-income and moderate-income households, including shelters for the homeless, community homes with built-in services, conventional rentals, limited equity co-operatives, limited equity condominiums, co-housing, and resale-restricted houses on leased land. The CHT's staff also provides a rich mix of services for homeowners and renters alike in order to help them succeed in the housing that is theirs and, when possible, to move along this continuum to achieve the type and tenure of housing that is best for them. These range from a broad array of financial education and counselling offerings for applicants seeking to rent, purchase or sustain their home through financial difficulty; direct social services and case management for those with special needs; and community building resident services like community gardens and youth programs. The CHT's most recent contribution to the region's housing needs is a partnership with the University of Vermont Medical Center Hospital to house people who are chronically ill and homeless. The hospital has contributed three million dollars in capital as well as operating subsidies for on-site health services, enabling the CHT to work towards its goal of eliminating chronic homelessness.

The CHT continues to be a leader in statewide housing coalitions in Vermont, and is heavily invested in the activities of Grounded Solutions Network (GSN), a membership organization made up of CLTs and other practitioners doing shared equity homeownership or co-operatives. GSN advocates for policy and funding specific to permanent affordability and provides technical assistance and training. In 2009, the CHT received the United Nations World Habitat Award for the Global North, recognizing the fiscal, environmental and social sustainability of CLT model. This brought international attention and acclaim for the CHT's distinctive approach to the decommodification of housing. As part of that the CHT hosted a site-study visit with participants from 13 countries, and spawned a number of CLTs with which the CHT continues to enjoy strong peer-to-peer relationships. These connections have helped to hasten the spread of the CLT model to other countries, including Australia, Belgium, the United Kingdom, and, more recently, Canada and France.

Brenda M. Torpy, Chief Executive Officer
Champlain Housing Trust

Acknowledgements

I would like to thank Erhard Mahnke for digging up details and fact-checking our memories about the development of co-operative housing in Vermont, John E. Davis for drastically editing and thus improving a much earlier version of this article, and Amy Wright for being a final reader. I am solely responsible for any errors that evaded their eagle eyes and encyclopedic knowledge of affordable housing.

To learn more about the Champlain Housing Trust, past and present: Champlain Housing Trust website: http://www.getahome.org/

REFERENCES

Davis, John Emmeus. 1994. 'Building the Progressive City: Third Sector Housing in Burlington'. In *The Affordable City: Toward a Third Sector Housing Policy*, 165–200. Philadelphia: Temple University Press.

Davis, John Emmeus, and Alice Stokes. 2009. *Lands in Trust, Homes That Last*. Burlington: Champlain Housing Trust.

Temkin, Kenneth, Brett Theodos, and David Price. 2010. *Shared Equity Homeownership Evaluation: Case Study of Champlain Housing Trust*. Washington, DC: The Urban Institute.

Torpy, Brenda. 2010. 'The Community Land Trust Solution: The Case of the Champlain Housing Trust'. In *Forging a New Housing Policy: Opportunity in the Wake of Crisis*, 64–66. Hempstead, New York: National Centre for Suburban Studies, Hofstra University.

1970 Architecture Canada Newsmagazine Debate

Architecture Canada Newsmagazine
July 20, 1970. Royal Architectural Institute of Canada

Urban Renewal
The "reactionary nonsense" of cherishing old buildings

It has been called "the largest and most imaginative private urban renewal redevelopment scheme ever attempted in Canada," it helped cause a split in one of the country's best-known architectural firms, and it has provoked a developer/tenant relationship that is at once both enlightened and bitter.

It's Montreal's proposed Cité Concordia, for which plans and models were shown to a star-studded group of local businessmen late last month. By the time it is finished, ten years from now, Cité Concordia will have cost some $250 million. It's to be a mixed commercial/residential development with 7,000 inhabitants.

Work will start this fall on the first phase. This has three principal elements: a 29-storey, twin-towered medical/office building; a 500-room hotel; and three "residential clusters" up to 25 storeys high and each wrapped around its own green "square."

Cité Concordia "has been conceived to stimulate human interaction around a contemporary village common," says a sumptuous brochure prepared by the developers. Cars and pedestrians are separated throughout the site. There are two pedestrian systems, one weather-protected and the other at surface level forming part of a network of landscaped squares, three "action centers" and walkways which could eventually plug into others similar in the city.

The question of how much should be preserved of what now stands on the 25-acre, six-block site has been a major source of controversy. Peter Desbarats, a respected Montreal journalist, describes it as "a somewhat dilapidated mixture of old apartment blocks, cheap boarding houses, nondescript churches and small stores. The population of 1,800 is 1/3 transient and a mosaic, in almost equal proportions, of English-speaking Canadians, Quebecers and immigrants. During the winter, students account for about 10% of the population. There is a small elite of professionals and intellectuals."

In the first phase, some 60 greystone townhouses plus a few old churches, schools and other buildings will be preserved. Says architect Dimitri Dimakopoulos: "The romantic notion that there's something mystically precious about a decaying building just because it happens to be 80 or 90 years old is one I don't share. A rat-infested, cockroach-ridden house in which the plumbing is falling apart and the electrical system is so antiquated it poses a fire hazard is hardly my idea of a home. People who favour that kind of housing for low-income families are talking nonsense—and reactionary nonsense at that."

For more than a year, the developer, Concordia Estates (Place Bonaventure etc.) has mounted a massive public relations program to sell its brave new world to the citizens it will displace. Although under no obligation to do so, the firm has paid generous relocation allowances to 50% of its 250 tenants in the first phase area. Most of the others have taken advantage of an alternative offer of accommodation elsewhere on the site at the same rent they have been paying. The hum of discontent seems to be dying down, and the way looks clear for a development that could be as significant as Place Ville Marie.

Architecture Canada Newsmagazine
September 14, 1970. Royal Architectural Institute of Canada.

OPINION
Opposing Montreal's super-project – Cité Concordia
Among the most vocal critics of Montreal's controversial Cité Concordia urban development scheme (see Architecture Canada July 20, 1970) has been architect Joseph Baker—a Royal Architectural Institute of Canada Fellow and a PQAA past president. We sent Baker a background kit on the project and asked him to explain to the other architects why he is so vehemently opposing the project. His reply:

Dear Madam Editor, you sent me a handsome publicity kit—ample text, glossy photographs and beguiling perspectives—all describing Montreal's superproject Cité Concordia, yet to be frank, I am not at all certain as to what you expect of me. An architectural critique? An assessment of environmental qualities? Should I share with my colleagues an anticipated pleasure of strolling through elegant Piazettas, of shopping in bustling Agoras, or note the meaningful urban statements, the intriguing sequential experience, the extraordinary sense of place? Or perhaps you would prefer something for the systems and technology buffs, with talk of soft and hard ware, "innovative components and pre-assemblies," "the intensive interdisciplinary interface" that the project represents?

If only I could oblige, but I regret that the Piazettas and Agoras "reminiscent of Europe" fail to excite me. Perhaps I fear that few Italians, Greeks or other European immigrants who have until now peopled the Park Avenue–St. Laurent district will survive their coming and the disappearance of the kind of accommodation and community that makes easier their entrance to a new country. Perhaps I'm too aware that the kind of enterprise that flourishes here belongs to folk who live over the store, work a grinding six day week and make out much like those they serve; has little to do with sophisticated indoor plazas, combined sales promotion and exotic design and that redevelopment for most means closing up and an early retirement. I honestly would like to believe "that the public squares and gardens throughout the project will act as gathering places for the same kind of people who give the neighbourhood its present flavour" but already, harassment by city police is pushing young people out ahead of the bulldozer. Architects may adorn their drawings with benches and planters but if experience at Alexis Nihon Plaza (much admired for its gathering and the more posh Westmount Square) is any indicator, blow torch removal and "no loitering" signs will terminate their use by people less perfect than the Holt Renfrew characters of Perspective land.

But perhaps this is but "reactionary nonsense." At least that's the way the developer sees it. "The romantic notion that there's something mystically precious about a decaying building just because it happens to be 80 to 90 years old is one I don't share," he states. Furthermore, "a rat-infested, cockroach-ridden house in which the plumbing is falling apart and the electrical system is so antiquated it poses a fire hazard is hardly my idea of a home." Worthy of Jacob Riis but spoken by the landlord, it's his own property the Board chairman is deploring. Admittedly they weren't acquired as homes, just real estate but one might question whether property can be held for ten years and allowed to become a hazard to the health and safety of its occupants. Just as one might question the massive buying drives involved in property acquisition, that create an artificial market level, drive up assessment and truly make it uneconomic for the new proprietor to hold existing rent scales and provide reasonable standards of maintenance.

It should be known that proprietors outside the Concordia field of interest achieve this latter feat because the cost of their obsolete housing has long since been amortised. This paid-up housing stock represents a valuable resource that mustn't get lost in the shuffle of the numbers game—pull down 500 put up 1,500 net gain 1,000, voila!—but its survival is precarious in a hostile environment. Zoning regulations that permit redevelopment to a density of twelve times the ground area amount to a declaration of year round open season on existing residential neighbourhoods. Rent subsidies no more than Public Housing will fill the void left by their disappearance. First call on public funds rightfully belongs to those in greatest need, which means families at or below the poverty level and in Quebec at least, they form a long line. But sustaining themselves in the older urban areas are what have been termed the affluent poor, unable to afford the high cost of new accommodation, unable to qualify for public assistance. As the Hon. Robert Andras succinctly put it, "These are the people who really get shafted in the redevelopment process." Their prospect, eat less, pay more rent and find a home in an area that in all probability is already the target of speculation.

Until the day dawns on effective legislation that will assure "all people, regardless of their economic status will be able to enjoy the same community amenities as their more fortunate neighbours," I opt for conservation, widespread rehabilitation and the maximum incentive for the development by dynamic enterprise and its equally dynamic architects, of vacant and misused city land. Rehabilitation, I'm aware, is open to interpretation. To the Toronto whitepainter, it means turning lead into gold; to the municipal housing bureaus, nothing of new house standards; to others it could just mean keeping in service shelter that people can afford—putting in a tub or even just hot water, insulation to cut down the heat bill or fixing the roof so the rain won't come in. It may not be "everybody's idea of a home but it will give the folk and their kids a break while we beef up on 'management systems and the interdisciplinary approach to construction.'"

So perhaps dear madam editor you will call on me again when, here in Montreal, we've got our priorities adjusted and our values untangled and I promise you a darling critique on say, the plumbing and patching of Pointe St. Charles. We'll have the Ford Foundation throw a Street Party, invite Bourassa and a virtual Who's Who of political, business, labour and community leaders, mingled (but of course) with neighbourhood residents.

Montreal and Boston: Intertwined Destinies

Julien Deschênes

WHEN ASKED TO contribute a chapter on Communauté Milton-Parc (CMP), I remembered my earliest introduction to it, crossing twice daily as a student at FACE School across from McGill. Living on the eastern side of CMP, these daily walks between 1998 and 2010 helped forge my interest in heritage, housing, community organization and community development—interests that eventually let to a career in urban planning. Similarly, my acquaintance with Dudley Neighbors Inc. (DNI), a community land trust (CLT) in Boston's Dudley neighbourhood, played a role as I got to know the area during summer vacations in Boston with my parents. As a master's student in urban planning at the Université de Montréal, I had the chance to study and visit DNI, discovering the ways in which the two communities shared similar pasts, presents, and destinies. This chapter is an attempt to highlight the Bostonian experience, exploring the links between the two organizations as well as the opportunities and challenges each face.

The Dudley Neighbors Inc.

DNI is a community land trust that creates accessible home ownership for low-income households, providing land for affordable housing co-ops, rental apartments, commercial units, parks and urban agriculture. It now has a portfolio of 225 affordable housing units that are permanently preserved from speculation by deeds and restrictions in a centrally-located neighbourhood of Boston.

To get a better understanding of where and how the Dudley neighbourhood came about, we need to set a few historical parameters. The neighbourhood was a white immigrant enclave until the 1960s and the 1970s when white residents fled to the suburbs. With their departure, the Black community became predominant and the area fell into a spiral of decline. The causes of this decline were multiple, with the loss of wealthier residents leading to vacant lots, city disinvestment and social segregation. The situation deteriorated when Black households and entrepreneurs were unable to access credit because of "redlining" practices by financial institutions. Redlining, banned by the American 1968 Fair

Housing Act, consisted of a discriminatory practice that denied access to services in specific areas based on their ethnic composition. As if this were not enough, the generalized abandonment left vacant properties to fall into disrepair with rampant dumping everywhere. Tires, garbage bags, and construction materials strewn about created the impression of a slum, while arson contributed to the general dereliction and air of decline.

As a result, the weakened community was left with no choice but to organize to gain control over the land it claimed as its own. People wanted to be able to invest in their community and create a place that would be perceived positively compared to the ghetto in the making. To this end, they formed the Dudley Street Neighborhood Initiative (DSNI) in 1984 to claim back neighbourhood control. This newly formed community organization became central in the fight by grassroots activists.

In 1985 the community structure began to take shape, with the election of a board and the first series of official meetings. A year later, DSNI hired its first staff and opened its office. With these new resources, they started campaigning against illegal dumping and organized neighbourhood cleanup activities to demonstrate a community presence. This became the stepping-stone to the 1987 participatory plan, the Dudley Street Neighbourhood Comprehensive Revitalization Plan. Through this plan, which was adopted by the city of Boston, they gained the power of eminent domain within an area named "The Triangle," so named because of its shape. This victory made them the only community organization within the United States capable of expropriating vacant land for public use. With the new powers gained in 1988, they put in place the DNI, which became the organization responsible for vacant parcels acquired from neglectful owners.

While at first this didn't seem to make much difference, the scale of abandonment and the lack of community control soon made it a powerful tool. The community land trust was able to evict owners that were neglecting their land and making it vulnerable to dumping and other undesirable activity. By gaining control over the land, the community became responsible for its own choices. The clean-up of the neighbourhood remained one of the primary concerns along with the creation of a community centre and housing units on the common ground held in trust by DNI. The efforts seemed to pay off when, in 1992, the land trust received a civic award from the city of Boston for best-kept neighbourhood. Passing from one of the most blighted neighbourhoods in the nation to best-kept in the city in less than a decade demonstrates the strength of DSNI and its ability to create a real sense of neighbourhood from scratch. That same year, they also started home buyer classes in anticipation of developing 36 affordable three-bedroom homes.

In 1994, one year after a victorious fight against the construction of an asphalt plant in the area, the first Winthrop Estate units were sold to households in what was to become a huge urban renewal process. This first tangible improvement was a meaningful demonstration that the neighbourhood was focused on creating a livable environment, in contrast to past decay and in the face of powerful economic interests. The Winthrop Estates' affordable units included three bedrooms and 1.5 bathrooms to accommodate families. For these units to remain affordable, DNI retained ownership of the land while each household became the owner of the unit built on it. This separation of property—the main component of land trusts—made sure the community still had a say regarding those lands by attaching deeds and restrictions aimed towards long-lasting affordability.

Through its structure, DNI oversees the deeds and restrictions through a board of directors including nine voting members and two non-voting members. Voting members include six members appointed by the DSNI board covering community organization needs and resident concerns, and three appointees from local officials from the neighbourhood, the district and the city. The two other non-voting seats are reserved for state senate and representative district appointees.

After the delivery of the Winthrop Estates and the acquisition of a commercial building to host a non-profit and a commercial tenant in 1994, the community started to introduce food production through the Food Project. The goal was to create a complete neighbourhood. The idea was not just to create a residential enclave, but to ensure residents also had access to jobs and healthy food. This request for more diverse functions took the shape of a farmer's market and a local business directory to guide the community, DNI, and DSNI in expanding this diversity. Moreover, the revitalization plan was updated in 1996 after almost nine years mostly left untouched and translating these new concerns into a community urban vision. The use of "what if" scenarios helped the community develop long-lasting approaches, thus strengthening the DNI model within the community structure.

From 1998 to 2001, 77 housing co-operative units and 31 home ownership units were inaugurated in three distinct projects. This three-year period marked the peak in housing production for DNI and a new way of separating property using the co-operative model. As with the home ownership units, the co-operative units are still divided two-ways, with DNI acting as the landowner and the operating co-operatives as the owners of the building and units. This major addition to DNI's portfolio justified its staffing by DSNI because residents and co-operatives needed support in many ways.

In the following years and until 2004, the DNI and DSNI organizations focused on youth and on secondary area residents. These new focuses appeared because of the emergent presence of youth community leaders (an increasing number since the DSNI was formed in 1984) and because of requests from residents from surrounding communities to be involved in the greater community. Accordingly, the organizations started to talk about an Urban Village and included secondary area residents to the DSNI board to enlarge its membership definition to a broader area. At the same time, multiple initiatives aimed towards greater opportunities for youth were developed due to the increasing numbers of young people in the community. This sudden attention to youth was galvanized by the death of 11-year old Trina Persad by a stray bullet in 2002. In 2004, the vacant lot where she died became the Trina Persad Park. The land underneath remained the property of the community through the DNI, and the DSNI youth's branch worked with artists in 2014 to create an art installation to keep her spirit alive.

The growth of both organizations is also visible throughout the period ranging from 2005 to 2015. These ten years saw the arrival of 52 new rental units, 24 home ownership units and approximately 5000 square-feet of commercial development, mostly due to the Dudley Village project, which was made possible by the Dorchester Bay Economic Development Corporation (DBEDC), a public arm of the City of Boston. The DBEDC developed this project, making sure to maintain its affordability and to ensure community control by handing ownership of the land to DNI through a donation. This transfer of property was central to the success of the Dudley experiment, even if it led to some tensions between organizations. In this specific case, the transfer led to a default of payment on the taxes that were due by the land trust to the city of Boston. The DBEDC, which retained ownership of the units, received a notice of this payment default, and had to pay the taxes on behalf of the DNI in order to maintain the property within the portfolio. In exchange, the DBEDC decided not pay their user's fees to redeem what they had to pay on behalf of the DNI. This situation led to some tension between the two organizations because of their mutual concern regarding the stewardship of the affordable units. After the settlement of the payment, this tension disappeared, but it raised awareness of potential threats to this model if organizations were not coordinated.

During this period, the sector also saw multiple urban agricultural initiatives breaking ground. Having access to community gardens was an early request from the residents; it became a reality in 2005 with the construction of the Dudley Greenhouse in partnership with The Food Project. This 10,000 square foot greenhouse was only made possible because the land was held in trust. This shows that having community control over land makes it feasible to convert this land in whatever way the community needs. After multiple housing developments, the residents decided that a complete neighbourhood needed to include public gardens where they could have access to fresh products. Providing the community with a greenhouse turned this ideal into a four-season reality. It was also difficult to create and justify a new field of expertise for DSNI and DNI, so the partnership with The Food Project played a structural role for this new type of activity, making it an instant success in the community. In addition to the greenhouse, a site transferred from the City of Boston to the DNI in 2013 became the West Cottage Farm. This urban farm was also cared for by The Food Project and helped nourish many Bostonians through local hunger relief organizations. By choosing urban agriculture over additional residential or commercial developments, the community addressed a collective problem and made sure to retain available land for that purpose.

Since all fairy stories have a darker side, a few elements were pointed out as problematic by the staff. The first administrators of DNI did not keep proper records on sales and resales. Missing key information still makes it impossible to depict a clear portrait of the evolution of their portfolio of units kept in perpetuity. The absence of clear rules and adequate counselling at the beginning also made some residents decide to keep their distance and even in some case develop mistrust towards the organizations. These negative perceptions of the administrators brought a group of longstanding residents to boycott a real estate tax rebate from the City of Boston that was negotiated by DNI.

The fear was that this rebate was a chimera invented by the trust. Unfortunately, these individual decisions to boycott became a handicap for these properties as new owners moved in. DNI was trying, in 2017, to renegotiate a rebate with the City of Boston on the properties that were not included in the first deal.

Another drawback resulting from their local, national and international success is their continuing attractiveness for researchers, local officials and those forming CLTs. Although the attention leads to the possibility of sharing the way they have implemented their model, those visits are coming on top of an already heavy workload. The presence of a high concentration of colleges and universities is pressuring the four employees that also have responsibilities in the DSNI team of 14 with intensive research and interviews. This concentration of scholars also brings a vast pool of potential interns and interesting research, such as the mapping impact analysis of DNI by Lee Allen Dwyer from MIT, in which he concludes that the neighbourhood could face two destinies: gentrification leading to displacement, or social fabric stabilization in tandem with the improvements.

What Now?

This year, after 30 years of operation, the DNI still plays an important role in this strong community. The current concern is focused on the Fairmount-Indigo railway, which became a big grassroots movement emerging from multiple community development corporations (CDC) in places where the railway runs.

This line used to be a commuter rail for suburbs, dividing neighbourhoods without servicing them properly because of expensive fares. In an effort to link those forgotten neighbourhoods to job centres, a collaborator with the CDCs decided to advocate for the use of this line to provide cheaper access to the transit system by adding freight volume and lowering fares for short distance riders. Those base requests were enhanced by the addition of environmental, economic development, local empowerment and development without displacement goals. All of them united in a precise development tendency: the transit-oriented development (TOD).

This TOD covers a vast sector of overlapping neighbourhoods in Boston, but Uphams Corner is the main station involving the Dudley group as it is at the outward limit of their area of service. Their interest is based on general community engagement and the efforts of the city of Boston, the Massachusetts Bay Transportation Authority (MBTA), and the Boston Planning and Development Agency (BPDA) to ensure development without affecting the social fabric of the neighbourhood.

The efforts towards the TOD project have involved the whole community in the joint acquisition of land and property to prevent displacement caused by upcoming development. However, the potential gain in mobility is as much of a threat as an opportunity for the people living and working in Uphams Corner. Trends are showing that the area is heating up because of the TOD. Acquisitions are made by the city to secure proper installation for upcoming projects such as a new public library branch, performance and rehearsal spaces, affordable housing and rooftop gardens. DNI, DSNI, and DBEDC are also invested in protecting the affordability and community control of the area. DNI and DSNI bought an old bank on the condition that whatever is held between the four walls remains affordable and accessible. DBEDC owns a building the corporation would like to renovate and make accessible to the community to fight the forces of gentrification that prevail in private ownership. Put together, these recent investments, public actions and general concern for the area contrast vividly with the abandonment that forced the creation of DSNI and DNI in the first place.

In the midst of this collective empowerment comes increased political influence in the highest spheres of Boston's municipal power. John Barros, the Chief of Economic Development in the mayor's office, was 15 when DNI took form. As a result, he has lived through the transformation of his neighbourhood. He also helped forge it as DSNI's Executive Director for 13 years. The national (and even international) attention to DSNI and DNI has contributed to setting the Bostonian community land trust on a pedestal.

This effervescence around the CLT made Barros a leading figure in the community development scene. Thus, it wasn't surprising that Mayor Martin J. Walsh appointed him in 2014 as chief of Economic Development. This nomination enhanced the influence of the neighbourhood by giving it an ally in a department of strategic importance.

Barros also arrived in his post during the transformation of the Boston Redevelopment Authority into the BPDA. The recent public investment and engagement with the neighbourhood are all the stronger as he still takes pride in living in Uphams Corner and says that home ownership is an essential part of his commitment to his community.

This urban leader, raised by his community and influenced by its waves of transformation, also engages in a different method of pursuing economic development. He defended the development of a Boston 2030 vision before competing for the Olympics. He said a clear vision for Boston is a prerequisite before submitting any candidacy for the Olympics, as this event either would or would not be an effective way to achieve this vision. This is a good example of how DNI and DSNI contribute to their community first and how they translate their ideas to a greater extent by a paradigm shift in the perception of urban development.

In doing so, the model appears to have entered a new reformist era, taking control of strategic spheres of power compared with its origins when the community was fighting both political and economic interests. The discourse about common ground forged over the past 30 years has evolved from that of a community whose interests centred around survival, development, and empowerment to that of a community focussed on fostering new paradigms in housing, economic development, community development and urban planning on a greater level. The DNI leadership in the Metro Boston Community Land Trust Network, launched in 2015, is further testimony to this paradigm shift initiated and fostered by the DNI and supported by DSNI. This might be the greatest legacy of those 30 years of community involvement and collective appropriation of a blighted neighbourhood.

Intertwined Pasts and Destinies

DNI emerged in a context where blight and abandonment were threatening the survival of a community, whereas CMP was organized around the secret manoeuvrings of developers and promoters looking to destroy the prevailing sense of community. But while the causes of the Bostonian community takeover differ from the ones that brought the first activists of CMP together, similarities between the two experiences can be found on multiple levels.

The most glaring one is probably the collective action towards the upkeep of a beloved neighbourhood. Both examples share a common concern about speculation, displacement and community control. By digging into both organizations' pasts, we find interesting correlations and oppositions that show that, despite similar goals, there are differences in application, and, despite different contexts, there is a similar social organization.

The involvement of the U.S. Ford Foundation is a good illustration of this paradoxical dichotomy. The withdrawal of this funding body from the Concordia Estates Ltd. project weakened the promoters and thus strengthened the Milton-Parc Citizens' Committee. In Boston, the funder played the opposite role but towards the same goal when he committed a 2 million USD low-interest loan to DNI for vacant land acquisition. This example of how a single actor played a determining role in the first stages of both organizations reveals the intertwined past shared by DNI and CMP. Let's address how we can trace a similar storyline characterized by multiple differences in the application of their respective models.

First of all, both organizations, through their collective structure, are facing administrative problems. Collective organizations with horizontal structures face tensions and moments of cold sweat. In their respective histories, we can find examples of personal tension and fights that common rules could have, or have already, addressed. The cold sweat moments are more interesting because they reveal the weaknesses of the organization. DNI revealed its weaknesses with the default in the tax payment, putting some hard-won gains at risk. Similarly, CMP revealed its own limits when it lost some commercial units through a tax default by its Société de Développement Communautaire Milton-Parc (SDC), the organization that manages the commercial properties in the CMP.

Taxes are not just a bad memory for the administrators; they also demonstrate the non-speculative merits of the two models. In Boston, the community land trust homeowners, who accepted the rebate from the city, benefit from a tax reduction in regard to the conditions and restrictions attached to their properties, especially the ones concerning the resale formula. Likewise, the Société d'amélioration Milton-Parc (SAMP), the precursor to MPC, contested the assessment value of the buildings to be transferred. This contestation found an echo at the Bureau de révision de l'évaluation foncière du Québec, when it stated in a decision that the assessed value should consider depreciation in accordance with the multiple deeds and restrictions attached to the properties. Those two tax-related events also contributed to the consolidation of shared concerns about a non-speculative model and continuous affordability.

In the same mindset, it is natural to underline that both organizations shared common goals, including housing access for low and moderate-income households, preserving the social fabric, and providing resale mechanisms to prevent speculation. In fact, one of the few points where the organizations diverged was that the architectural and heritage preservation so fundamental to the success of CMP was not a factor in driving the mandate of DNI, where the focus was explicitly on urban renewal.

Like CMP, DNI is essentially residential but has a majority of owner-occupied properties that are tied to a resale formula, with multiple conditions and restrictions regarding the occupancy and initial access to the properties. CMP decided to go for a co-operative model where residents collectively share ownership of the land and units, while DNI splits the property in two and remains the owner of the land while leaving the units to homeowners under strict conditions. The resale formula designed by DNI leaves a share of 25% of the capital gain to the owner, while the remaining 75% is reinvested in DNI's mission to expand and protect its portfolio, thus encouraging the expansion of affordable and non-speculative opportunities over time. Even if this model promotes independent growth of the portfolio, the massive public investments in CMP secured 616 affordable housing units, representing almost 274% more units than DNI.

In terms of commercial units and activity, the CMP also seems more productive with its SDC even though it had to let go of some units to survive. The CMP also went beyond its counterpart by stimulating commercial activity with CMP's own commercial organizations, while DNI teamed-up with local business and community groups. The Bostonian experiment on the commercial level seems more stable and resilient.

The two non-profit organizations also contributed to their urban environment by increasing the sense of safety and by providing public spaces, parks and community gardens. Both neighbourhoods increased their amounts of green space and public space through community pressure and common ownership of strategic pieces of land. The co-operative and community land trust models reveal a great ability and efficiency to transform the neighbourhoods into something that looks like the community that lives on it. Both cases demonstrate, through multiple examples, how the collective engagement towards embellishment and greening seems natural with a collective responsibility over land. Thus, the optimization of the land, in comparison to private speculative ownership, is not an economic calculus but a social consideration. In addition to those embellishments and greening initiatives, it is also possible to observe a shift towards a more secure neighbourhood. In the case of DNI, it translates into programs for youth, including the commemoration of Trina Persad through a park. In Montreal, the reality is different, but the increased sense of security has undergone physical improvements, like the destruction of the Pine-Parc interchange and the closure of Hutchison Street for the benefit of pedestrians, cyclists and residents.

The comparison of both organizational structures reveals one major difference: DNI's board is tripartite and includes elected officials from the city of Boston, residents, and other members from the service area. This structure opens the organization and its residents up to the outside, thus engaging a broader community which doesn't specifically benefit from the organization. It creates transparency and social cohesion with other stakeholders directly concerned in the issues discussed. This involvement is a commitment towards a larger group of residents and stakeholders affected by the decisions and well being of DNI because of their physical proximity.

In both cases, the social organization existed before the chosen non-speculative vehicle. In Boston, residents formed the DSNI, while in Montreal the Citizens' Committee formed the SAMP. The high number of professionals among the residents (urban planners, architects, community organizers, social workers, lawyers and representative from the business world) in its early days is distinctive to Montreal, as the Dudley neighbourhood initially appeared less professional in nature. DNI was created to become the steward of the firsts units of housing produced, whereas in Montreal the CMP came after the production of the housing co-ops' constellation. Those elements of timing probably contributed to the structure of the models and their respective evolution over time.

Finally, another resemblance between the two organizations is the acknowledgement of their successes. Both received high distinction and recognition of their work. However, this success is not guaranteed in the future and they need to remain flexible, open and resilient to embrace the challenges of tomorrow. After decades of community involvement regaining control over the land, they made sure to protect it from speculation but in doing so they also contributed to increased pressure on their surrounding environment by creating livable neighbourhoods. What initially made these neighbourhoods attractive for professionals in Montreal and the white immigrants of Dudley is starting to, or has already, reappeared; and market pressure could affect the surrounding areas, especially where urban opportunities are emerging, as at Upham's Corner in Boston, or with the vocational changes of big institutions such as the Royal-Victoria and Hôtel-Dieu hospitals in Montreal.

Both CMP and DNI will have a role to play to make sure that gentrification on one side won't displace the community and its residents, and that strategic heritage and public infrastructure on the other remain part of the public realm. The 30th anniversary of both organizations, combined with these great challenges, represents unprecedented momentum. The credibility, knowledge and land parcels gained through the years could be useful tools to leverage an expansion of the respective missions. Such an expansion could allow more people to benefit from well-structured, non-speculative models and go beyond traditional community organization by introducing a real paradigm shift in the way we experience our living environments. Therefore, CMP and DNI could use the multilevel leverage gained through the years to expand community control of the land or at least actively assist other community groups in that regard. The interest of CMP in the Hôtel-Dieu and the actions taken by DNI in Upham's Corner are the living proofs of the community spirit that grew through the years and the confirmation that their destinies are full of hopeful promise.

REFERENCES

Crimaldi, Laura. 2018. 'How the City Plans to Beat Gentrification in Uphams Corner'. *Boston Globe*, 12 February 2018.

'Dudley Neighbors, Inc.'. n.d. Dudley Neighbors, Inc. Accessed 17 October 2018. http://www.dudleyneighbors.org/.

'Dudley Street Neighborhood Initiative'. n.d. DSNI. Accessed 17 October 2018. https://www.dsni.org/.

Dwyer, Lee Allen. 2015. 'Mapping Impact: An Analysis of the Dudley Street Neighborhood Initiative Land Trust'. Master in City Planning, Massachusetts Institute of Technology, Department of Urban Studies and Planning. https://dspace.mit.edu/handle/1721.1/98934.

Fairmount Indigo Community Development Corporation Collaborative. n.d. 'Home'. *Fairmount Indigo*. Accessed 17 October 2018. http://fairmount collaborative.org/.

'John Barros'. n.d. Boston.Gov. Accessed 17 October 2018. https://www.boston.gov/departments/economic-development/john-barros.

Kowaluk, Lucia, and Carolle Piché-Burton. 2012. *Communauté Milton-Parc: How We Did It and How It Works Now*. Montréal: Communauté Milton-Parc.

Woolhouse, Megan. 2014. 'Seven Things You Should Know about John Barros'. *Boston Globe*, 19 October 2014. https://www.bostonglobe.com/business/2014/10/18/seven-things-you-should-know-about-john-barros-boston-chief-economic-development/BOboEtfwnT4dZ5K7YtWNSI/story.html.

Spring-Summer 1971
BULLDOZER: Bulletin of the MPCC

BULLDOZER
MILTON PARK CITIZENS COMMITTEE
Vol. 3 No. 2 April 71

They enter the neighbourhood under false names. Through stealthy conspiracy, they gain control over the unsuspecting people. When protest finally emerges against their dictatorial powers, they say all their actions are justified by their plan for a new world.

Maoists? Communists? No—"Reds"—Real Estate Developers.

Concordia bought up their six blocks using various names, consulting nobody, following a plan to deprive hundreds of people of their homes and their neighbourhood.

Soon Concordia will have the company of other REDs. The International Real Estate Federation is holding its conference here, April 25–29. One thousand, seven hundred realtors, from 26 countries, will be wheeling and dealing, wining and dining, at the Queen Elizabeth Hotel.

And Norman Nerenberg, president of Concordia Estates, who is doing all he can for urban ruin, will speak on "urban renewal."

The world's real estate men have a lesson to learn. They aren't the only ones who can wheel and deal. Neighbourhoods can act too.

When the real estate men come to Montreal, let Nerenberg talk about his futile plans. Milton-Park will show them what neighbourhood action can do.

Why Stop Concordia?

The main goal of the Milton-Park Citizens' Committee for the near future is to stop Concordia Estates Co. from demolishing our neighbourhood. The committee has been fighting this company for almost three years, to save the community. There have been lots of little battles in the bigger war, and we have won most of them. Milton-Park is still here!

Our neighbourhood is made up of French, English, Greek, Portuguese, and other European and Asian immigrants. It is an area with many families and a considerable number of young people and senior citizens. The people in Milton-Park are not rich. Statistics show that the people here tend to stay here longer than in other parts of the city. They also show that the average income is lower than for the City of Montreal. The houses are big in Milton-Park. It is not difficult to find 8 or 9 room apartments in our neighbourhood, for reasonable rents. This is what Concordia wants to destroy. Where now you can find an 8 room apartment for $125 or less, Concordia wants to tear it down and build bachelor, 1 room apartments for $180 and more.

If we cannot stop Concordia, the people who live in Milton-Park will have to leave. A community will be destroyed. And, people like them—immigrant, French-Canadian, low-income, and families—will not replace them. But the rich, unmarried or childless, the passing student, the professional on his way to the suburbs, will climb up to his bachelor high-rise apartment and look down on what used to be a neighbourhood.

The long-term goal of the committee is to help other neighbourhoods save themselves from threats like Concordia, because the same thing will happen everywhere in Montreal. There are people, powerful people, who want to turn everything into money, and that includes you, and your neighbourhood, and your kids. That's why, for example, they throw 2000 people out of their homes to build a highway nobody wants. That's why Concordia must be stopped. Not just to save Milton-Park, but to strengthen the resistance to the destruction of the neighbourhood for money.

You can help do that. Talk about what Milton-Park is doing. Tell anybody, everybody. Talk about Concordia's plan to tear down good houses. Tell everybody. Talk about that lousy East-West autoroute when you're shopping, working, or at Church. Tell your children. Do what you can—all the time.

BULLDOZER
Bulletin of Milton-Park Citizens' Committee
[undated, but circa July 1971]

Can We Build a New Community Together?

The Milton-Park Citizens' Committee was established in 1968 when it was learned that a large section of the area was facing imminent destruction. Then, as now, the cry was "STOP CONCORDIA." But our activities have never had the negative basis suggested by this slogan. We have not worked just with the vision of preserving what exists here and now (or did three years ago—witness the boarded-up stores and houses). One of our lines of attack has been to build the Milton-Park area into a vital, healthy, attractive and inexpensive place in which to live. This is not to say that we have not been misled in these goals by the pressures of the situation facing us or that we have always faced the difficulties in which we find ourselves. But we think that our goals are worthwhile and that our hopes are not without some justification.

What's Bugging Us?

Our community has very many difficult problems to face if it is to survive and to become the kind of place in which we would like to live. We have to meet the challenge of the high-rise "filing cabinets" that many of us do not want to live in and that most of us cannot afford. We have to face the fact that our homes are just not economically viable with the tax load placed on this area in order to pay for Expo 67, the Olympic Games, etc. We are living in a city which places capitalists' profits and political personality cults ahead of our health, our social services, our comfort and our environment.

Many of the houses in this area are not in excellent condition, especially those belonging to Concordia (a coincidence?). What can we do about it without tearing apart the social fabric which unites us? Cité Concordia is obviously not the answer. It has already closed down our stores and some of our homes. It will dislocate us, crowd us into an even smaller area, increase our property taxes and only worsen the already serious situation that exists here.

And there are many other problems which we, as a community, must try to solve such as a lack of adequate health services, laundromats, etc.

Part of the Whole?

Many of the problems above are not just our problems, but the problems of the larger society of which we are a part. And we cannot solve our problems without dealing with these problems as well. Even if we stop Concordia, there will be other Concordias and other tentacles to oppress us.

The Milton-Park Citizens' Committee has been providing a number of services to the residents of this area—Family Clinic, Community Workshop, etc. And they have not always been as successful as we would like. We do not feel that it is our responsibility to provide these services, but we hope the community as a whole will become aware of what its real needs are and what prevents the fulfillment of these needs. These services are your responsibility. The government is too busy looking after the needs of corporate enterprise to be really interested in us.

There is a future but you have to make it!

Inner-City Youth Project

Teenagers in this community have very particular problems. Not many have enough money to frequent recreational facilities, municipal or otherwise. As a result, many find themselves out on the streets from morning until night, trying to find something to do.

The Inner-City Youth Project directs itself at the resolution of this problem. We do not have office hours and appointments. Instead, we are out on the streets in the community, making friends, contacts and plans. Once a worker finds a group of teenagers, he "hangs around" until a sufficiently high trust level is achieved. Then, together, worker and youths, apply themselves to the problems of the group.

Tours to the General Motors' plants do not interest us. Our primary aim is to open up community resources for the general use of the community. For example, some of the people with whom we came in contact expressed a desire to go swimming. Where could we go? For free? Sitting around talking about it, someone suggest that we could perhaps use the pool in the High School of Montreal. We asked for this pool and we got it. The kids started to get the idea. One went to the First Presbyterian Church on Jeanne Mance St. and obtained the use of a finished night-club style basement room called the coal bin. Now we have weekly performances, music and fun there. Another teenager went to St. James United Church—now we have the use of a three-lane bowling alley twice a week. The Devonshire School Parents' Committee is lending us their baseball equipment. We have cosom hockey at the University Settlement. Two groups are making candles and wax sculpture. Camping trips and outings to beaches are organized. We have films and discussions. A task force is helping out at the church day camp and doing construction work on the playground of Devonshire School.

We have an independent headquarters and restricted program area at 3649 Jeanne Mance St. The young people here run everything from finances to janitorial work. Everyone has fun and, at the same time, learns to look upon this community and all the resources in it as their own and to demand the right to use them.

A Co-operative Laundromat?

A fire closed down the "Good 'N Fast Washeteria" on Milton St. near Park Ave. in early June 1971. There is now a desperate need for a laundromat in the Milton-Park area. The Milton-Park Citizens' Committee, which had been trying to improve the lousy laundromat situation earlier this year, got active on the problem again. We have never approached funding sources for money and we are looking for a good place so that we can set up a co-operative laundromat. If we can do this, residents of the Milton-Park area will be both owners and clients of the laundromat. They will be able to decide all policies of their own service—hours, personnel, décor, etc. Eventual profits from the laundromat will be used to purchase such things as drugs for the medical clinic and supplies and equipment for the community workshop. Further news about this will appear in the Bulldozer.

Give Us Back our Stores!

It had been quite a while since the Milton-Park Citizens' Committee had made itself visible to the people in the area. It had also been quite some time since the Committee had publicly taken a stand against Concordia Estates Ltd. and other high-rise developers. Some kind of action was necessary to change this.

We had a ready-made issue at hand: the closure during past months and years of approximately twenty local shops and services on Park Ave. between Milton St. and Pine Ave. Why did the shop-keepers leave these stores? Most of the shop-keepers were on a month-to-month lease from Concordia and, therefore, at any time, they could be given thirty days' notice to vacate the premises. This uncertainty made it very difficult for stores like the hardware to build up a large inventory. Understandably, the shop-keeper did not want to be left with thousands of dollars worth of stock when he did not know where, or even if, he could find another store.

The people who live in the Milton-Park area are unhappy about the closure of the stores for several reasons. Many of the boarded-up stores used to be community gathering places—one would often bump into friends and neighbours there. In a number of the stores, a personal relationship had developed over the years between shopkeeper and customer. People miss this personalized service. Also, there are many elderly people living in the area who find it difficult to walk all the way to St. Lawrence to buy nails or to do their laundry. For them, the closure of the stores has been a source of real hardship. As well, most Milton-Park residents do not own cars so they can't easily travel in downtown Montreal to get the goods and services which were once within walking distance of their homes.

The Milton-Park Citizens' Committee wanted to dramatize the fact that Concordia, by creating an air of uncertainty in the area, had forced many shop-keepers to close up their stores and, if possible, the Committee wanted to force Concordia to reopen the stores. Committee members hoped to engage in an imaginative action which would attract people and, at the same time, convey this message.

And so, on Saturday June 26th, 1971, at 1 P.M. about twelve members of the Committee, dressed in white coats and wearing "STOP CONCORDIA" signs stationed themselves in front of several boarded-up stores near the corner of Prince Arthur St. and Park Ave. Representing shop-keepers who had been forced to vacate their stores, they handed out various symbolic objects, each with a message attached to it, to people walking by. Anti-Concordia Survival Water and Q-Tips were given away at the pharmacy, apples at the old grocery store, nails at the hardware, a shoe repair ticket at the cobbler's old shop, and a bag of detergent at the laundromat.

At what was once the post-office, people were asked to sign a petition and a letter protesting the closure of stores on Park Ave. and accusing Concordia of deliberately attempting to destroy the heart of the Milton-Park community. People mailed the letter to Concordia on Saturday, thereby registering their dissatisfaction. The petition, which was signed by more than 150 people, was sent to the elected representatives of the Milton-Park area at the municipal, provincial and federal levels of government.

The police, on this occasion sympathetic and friendly, were present to witness the June 26th action, as was Mr. Norman Nerenberg, General Manager of Concordia. There were also many reporters and photographers present which resulted in excellent coverage of the event by radio, press and T.V.

Most people seemed sympathetic to what the Committee was trying to do on June 26th. In all, we successfully conveyed our political point to the public and we had a lot of fun doing it.

April 1972
Community Press
Milton Park Community Press, formerly *The BULLDOZER*

The COMMUNITY PRESS is published every month to two months by the Milton Park Citizens' Committee. The paper seeks the participation of all members of the community at any level. The content and views expressed herein are the responsibility of an independent editorial collective for this issue made up of Bruce Roberts, Henry Milner, Jean-Claude Clari, Dimitri Roussopoulos, Kevin Cohalon, Jimmy Kelly and Paul-Emile Hains.

Others who helped were Louis Hall, Don Nemiroff, Mrs. Kemp, Cassie Gottlieb.

Squat-In Planned

After four years of opposition to the Cité Concordia development plan, Milton-Park Citizens' Committee has decided to force Concordia's hand by direct action. With the help of outside sympathetic organizations such as the Association des Locataires Metropolitan, Milton-Park is planning to occupy the closed housing units in the centre of the area until a satisfactory answer is received from the City and Concordia.

On February 5, 1972, a demonstration was held around the closed houses demanding they be opened and renovated for public use. A press conference was held afterward in which the Citizens' alternative plan for the area was launched. The plan proposed that the City ask for a Canada Mortgage and Housing Corporation (CMHC) loan such that a non-profit citizens' corporation would eventually own and control the housing. A meeting was subsequently held with Mr. John Lynch-Staunton of Executive Committee of the City of Montreal who declared that the City supported the Concordia project and until it had officially collapsed, would continue to support it. The City has already helped Concordia by granting it considerable tax relief.

In the face of city obstinance and Concordia's stand-pat attitude, Milton-Park decided to plan a squat-in of the closed houses if no action is forthcoming before an April 15 deadline. Two general assemblies have been held in which other concerned groups participated. Sympathetic residents of the quartier are invited to give their support to the occupation action and to attend meetings of the Milton-Park Citizens' Committee held regularly on Tuesdays at 8 p.m. at 3553 Saint-Urbain where strategy will be discussed.

Direct Action

The direct action being organized needs the active assistance of hundreds of people. There will be those who will occupy the house, there will be those who do the repairs, who will paint, who will speak to their friends and neighbours about the direct action, those who will provide food for the squatters, and household goods, who will donate money, who will speak to the newspapers, radio and television. Others will come to visit the squatters in the empty houses, to wish them good luck, others who will form a supporting peaceful demonstration in front of the occupied houses. If Concordia Estates Ltd. tells the police to arrest the squatters in the houses, the squatters will need our further support. Demonstrations will have to be organized that will show that we are with them all the way.

This action is a community action, we must all support it, otherwise we are saying that we don't care, and when the bulldozers come to carry out their work of destruction, and when we walk our neighbourhood streets that will look like bombed-out lots for some films we have seen from World War II, then it will be too late.

There are many things to be done. Everybody's help is important. Let us all defend our community together.

Why Direct Action

Citizens in our immediate community have been concerned for some time about the fact that in a city which does not have enough housing for people with reasonable rents, and large families, we walk down streets with houses that are boarded up scheduled to be demolished. These houses were homes that were warm, large, comfortable. They are not the little box apartments that people are forced to live in nowadays. But because the high-rise apartments make more profits for landlords, and more taxes for the municipal government, our neighbourhood is going to be destroyed by landlords and politicians. It is not only the grand old houses that are going to be destroyed, our very lives are going to change. The rents will go up, the shops are going to increase their prices, our friends will be forced to move out, our streets will change their character. Nothing will be the same again. While in other cities people are valuing more and more what is old, and seek to restore old houses which represent a way of life that we now long for rather than the crowded way of life of today, we in Montréal have a set of landlords and politicians ready to destroy in the name of "progress." Their "progress" will mean more pollution, more overcrowding, more running around madly to make a dollar, more high-rise ugly buildings that soon look shabby because they are so badly and cheaply made.

Many people in our community have organized themselves to prevent our neighbourhood from being destroyed. They have said why not repair, rebuild, paint, improve, restore, rather than destroy and build something new that in 10–15 years will look shabby again. It is a whole attitude to life, to community, to social responsibility that divides us from these politicians and landlords.

Many people in our community have thus signed petitions addressed to politicians, held peaceful demonstrations, organized press conferences, got some publicity in the newspapers, radio and television.

Then our fellow citizens along with architects and town-planners who had the same approach to life, the same social values set out to design an alternative plan for restoring, rebuilding and repairing our community. The plan was very well done, students in architecture drew all the designs, it was very impressive. The plan was taken to the politicians, the politicians in the municipal government, in the Québec government, in the Federal government, the bureaucrats in the various government agencies. More press conferences, more radio, television and newspaper publicity and more peaceful demonstrations. The answers were, "Maybe," "But," "Perhaps," "Wait and see," and so on, and so on.

Meanwhile, our neighbourhood is going downhill, there are 250 houses boarded up, there are stores that have been closed for years. We want our community to take a new step towards life, we want our community to serve the needs of working people and the poor. We want the houses open, with low rents, socially owned, and we want the shops open serving the needs of the people. And we want this now! No more waiting!

Who then can appropriate to himself the right to destroy in order to profit, without committing a flagrant injustice? Who then has the right to sell or destroy to any bidder the smallest portion of our common work and our common heritage?

Those who have watched at all closely the growth of certain ideas among ordinary people must have noticed that on one momentous question—the housing of people—a consensus is beginning to emerge. This idea in the minds of people is, and nothing will ever convince them otherwise again, that the "rights of property" ought not to extend to houses.

Those closed houses were not built by their owners. They were erected, decorated and furnished by innumerable workers, in the timber yard, the brick field, and the workshop, toiling for dear life at an inadequate wage.

The money spent by the directors of Concordia Estates Ltd. was not the product of their own labour. It was amassed, like all other riches, by paying the workers two-thirds or only half of what was their due.

Moreover—and it is here that the enormity of the whole proceeding becomes most glaring—these closed houses owe their actual value to the profit which the owners can make of them. Now, this profit results from the fact that these houses were built in a city possessing bridges, schools, hospitals, and affording to its citizens a thousand comforts, which is the work of many generations.

A house in Montréal may be valued at thousands of dollars not because thousands of dollars worth of labour have been expended on that particular house, but because it is in Montreal and because for over a hundred years workmen, artists, thinkers and men of learning have contributed to make Montreal what it is today—a centre of industry, commerce, art and science.

SO WE ARE GOING TO OPEN THE HOUSES OURSELVES, with the homeless and poor. We are going to do this by means of direct action. That is, we are going to open the houses ourselves, occupy them, repair them, paint them, and help people who need them to live in them.

The direct action will involve the people who need houses like these, and those people who support them. There are families with problems, whose basic problem is that they haven't got a proper home. That's the problem from which many other problems stem, and we want to help them solve it.

Everything else that our politicians expect of us has been tried.

The squatters have two simple aims—to do what they can in a few houses, and to encourage other people to do what they can in other empty houses. The first priority is direct action—to get some people in need of proper homes into empty houses by their own efforts; the second priority is to spread the news of what has been done rather than by talk, talk, talk of what might be done.

Milton Park Community Press, (formerly *The BULLDOZER*)
Vol. 1 No. 2 special issue!, June 1972
59 PEOPLE ARRESTED. *ACTIONS CONTINUE*
On Friday, May 29, 1972, fifty-nine members of the Milton-Park Citizens' Committee were arrested at the office of Concordia Estates Ltd. for protesting the demolition of low-cost housing in their community. Sixteen people occupied the office at 3553 Park Avenue, declaring that they would not leave until they had spoken with Norman Nerenberg, President of Concordia Estates Ltée. The Concordia office staff went into a panic, held consultations, made phone calls and finally advised the citizens that it was impossible for Mr. Nerenberg to leave his office at Place Bonaventure. Further, if the citizens did not leave the premises quietly and immediately, they would face arrest. The occupiers chose to remain.

Outside, approximately sixty demonstrators were picketing against Concordia's policies of bulldozer development. The people were addressed by Emile Boudreau of the Montreal Labour Council and Michel Bourdon of the Confederation of National Trade Unions, as well as by representatives of social agencies and community groups. The speakers expressed their support for the Committee's resistance to corporate destruction of their community and to the City of Montreal's complicity in this destruction.

About half an hour before any arrests were made, approximately thirty policemen gradually encircled the demonstrators in front of the Concordia office, refusing many people the right to leave. The first demonstrators loaded into the paddy wagon were not given any warning or option to leave. When a police captain finally gave the order to disperse, several people who tried to do so were arrested anyway. These people are all presently charged with ASSAULT.

Police then entered the Concordia office to remove the occupiers who resisted passively and who had to be carried into the waiting paddy wagon. Men, particularly long-hairs, received the roughest treatment. On arrival at Police Station No. 4 (Ontario and Saint-Dominique streets), this paddy wagon was stationed, with its doors closed, in the hot sun. Its occupants had to suffer extreme heat and lack of fresh air while the other demonstrators were being processed inside the station.

Conditions of Detention:

Female Prisons

The female prisoners, after having answered some routine questions at the registration desk in Station No. 4, were led into a ten foot by ten foot stone wall cell which had only a two foot by two foot grill window, leading into a small corridor. For the next five hours (from 4:30 p.m. to 9:30 p.m.) twenty-four women were kept in these cramped and dirty quarters without anything to eat or drink. One of the women, a nursing mother, was suffering from engorged breasts. It took more than an hour of pounding on the cell door and yelling "Au secours!" to get the police to release this woman.

At 9:30 p.m. the women were transferred by paddy wagon from Station N°. 4 to Station N°. 1 (rue Bonsecours) where police matrons searched them and then led them into a large common room. Here they had something to eat and they were able to make telephone calls to their lawyers, as well as to family and friends. At first, the women refused to be fingerprinted, but, after consulting with their lawyer, Bernard Mergler, they agreed to submit to this procedure. At 2:30 in the morning the first women were taken to be fingerprinted, photographed and to answer questions concerning their family, their use of alcohol and drugs, etc. The last woman was released from Station No. 1 at 4:15 a.m., twelve hours after the arrests took place. In spite of the callous treatment the female prisoners received at the hands of the police, feelings of solidarity remained strong among the women.

Male Prisoners
At Police Station N°. 4 the thirty-five male prisoners were booked, searched and had their personal belongings, including glasses, belts and wallets, removed. Like the women, the men were put in cramped quarters, but they were not kept together in one group. Instead, they were placed in five different cells so that the men in one cell were effectively isolated from the men in the other cells. In one cell a man was suffering from a kidney stone attack. As the severity of this attack became obvious to the other men in the cells, they attempted to attract police attention by banging on the walls and yelling in unison. This eventually brought a police officer who scornfully declared, "If he was sick, he should have stayed home." No medical attention was provided for this man at any time during his detainment.

At 10:00 p.m. the male prisoners were moved from Station No. 4 to Station No. 1. Here they were finally given sandwiches and coffee and, after a tedious process of fingerprinting, mugshots, and questioning, they were released. The last male prisoner left Station No. 1 at 2:30 in the morning. At no time were the men allowed to make phone calls nor were they give any news of what was happening on the outside. The whole affair was a good lesson in the double standard of bourgeois democracy and showed clearly what rights people actually do have once they are in police custody.

On their release from jail, all fifty-nine citizens were met by friends in cars and were taken back to the University Settlement. There food and supporters of the Milton-Park Citizens' Committee were waiting. And now we have a court case on our hands. On Wednesday, June 14 at 10:00 a.m. the "Milton-Park 59" will appear in Municipal Court to face charges of common assault.

7 DAYS IN MAY
A chronicle of the struggle against Concordia

After four years of opposition to the proposed Cité Concordia project, the Milton-Park Citizens' Committee has finally come to life. Faced with the immediate threat of demolition of the enclosed houses in the core of the community, at least 100 people are waging an active struggle to prevent Concordia Estates Ltd. from continuing with its present plans.

Over two months of work have gone into the preparation of this action. Members of the committee have spent time talking to hundreds of people in the neighbourhood. Citizens' committees, trade unions and social agencies throughout Montreal have been contacted and almost without exception have supported the activities of the committee in its attempts to have their alternate plans for the community implemented. But the real impetus for the present actions came from the initiation of demolition of one of the closed houses at the corner of Prince Arthur and Park Avenue.

Here is how events have shaped up over the last two weeks:

MAY 19. One day before a planned demonstration Concordia announced that demolition had begun. Workmen from the A.B.C. Demolition Company began preliminary work.

MAY 20. The next morning 150 people participated in a demonstration to protest the demolition. They paraded through the streets and around the closed houses waving placards and chanting slogans such as "Houses are for People" and "Ouvrons les Maisons." At the point where the marchers were passing the house being demolished a number of people broke in and immediately began a symbolic renovation. Paint, brushes, mops and pails appeared from all over the neighbourhood. Boards were removed from windows and used to make furniture. An electrical system was hooked up. By evening everyone was settled in comfortably.

MAY 21–22. The next two days passed with the residents of the "liberated" house doing further renovation work. A group of people who were without homes arrived to share the new accommodations. Animated discussions were a common sight, both in the house and on the street, as people from the community dropped by to tour the newly opened house and to see what was happening.

People were very surprised to find that the apartments that were opened were in such good condition. Except for the lack of water and plumbing they could have been made into very comfortable homes for anyone. The committee was renewed in its belief that these houses should be renovated and not demolished.

On Monday night, in anticipation of the workmen returning to work, a large meeting was held to discuss strategy.

MAY 23. About 80 people were on hand at 6:30 Tuesday morning to form a human chain in front of the house in order to demonstrate to the workmen that people did not want to see the centre of the Milton-Park community reduced to a pile of rubble. However, at 7:00 a.m. the Montreal police riot squad arrived on the scene and, after negotiations, cleared the demonstrators from the front of the house and removed eight squatters who had remained inside.

People immediately assembled to discuss further tactics. The rest of the morning was spent talking to the workmen who appeared very sympathetic. With their cooperation the remainder of the furniture was removed from the house.

Then at 1:00 p.m. a picket went up in front of the house and a number of people occupied another house across the street. The police then gave the occupiers until 6:00 p.m. to vacate the premises. After some discussion it was decided to avoid a confrontation at that point and to direct further efforts against Concordia and not against the demolition company.

MAY 24–25. During the next two days the efforts of the committee were directed towards preparing a petition and beginning a door-to-door campaign to talk to people in the community.

Then on Thursday night a group of people visited the home of Mr. Norman Neremberg, president of Concordia, to invite him to our next action.

MAY 26. The next action took place on Friday afternoon when a number of people occupied the Concordia rental Office on Park Avenue. They were supported by a crowd of sympathizers on the street outside. This action resulted in the arrest of 59 people, all of whom have been charged with common assault (See accompanying story).

The people involved in these actions are resolved to continue the struggle using every possible means to preserve and develop the Milton-Park community. Their efforts are continuing.

Hunger Strike!

On June 9, members of the M.P.C.C began a hunger strike. They are making the following demands:
1. That all demolition in the Milton Park area be stopped,
2. That a committee be set up to use the Milton Park alternate plan (see People's Power section) as a basis for the renovation of the closed houses,
3. That charges against the 59 persons be dropped
   The Conseil de Développement Social, a grouping of Montreal citizens' groups, has supported the action unanimously.

Financial Report on Concordia

The financial history and present situation of the Concordia group is almost as unknown as it is unsound. There are at least 38 different corporations in the Concordia group, dating back to 1952. The mother company is Concordia Estates Holding Ltd. under which there are five corporations who share not only the Concordia name but also many of the same officers. The major figures in this group are: Arnold Issenman, the original leader who is reputedly attempting to extract himself from the group; Norman Neremberg, a former treasurer of the Communist Party of Quebec, who, upon his "disillusionment" in 1957, was invited into the partnership and is presently head of the Cité Concordia Project; Q.L. Carlson, a relatively recent addition, who played a major role in both the Place Ville Marie and the Place Victoria development, K.G. Perry; N. Weisbord; T.M. Phelan; and J. Guy Gauvreau, apparently the token in the firm, needless to say he is President of the holding company.

The Concordia performance record is a varied one. The group's first major project was in Chateauguay where, in a 500 house development, they just broke even. The group then started the Place Bonaventure project, the financing of which has had a direct influence on the Cité Concordia development. The first 50 million dollars of the mortgage was split by Great West Life Assurance Co. (55%) and the Montreal Trust Co. (45%). When it became apparent that an additional $30 million was needed, the Montreal Trust co. was committed elsewhere and so the G.W.L.A. Co. picked it up in the form of short-term debentures. The ensuing years of mismanagement and hence low profit margins ended up with the Assurance Co., gaining equity control (i.e. ownership). On November 8, 1969, after it had become public knowledge that Place Bonaventure was behind in taxes to the tune of $1,673,998, the Financial Post informed Canadian business circles that "spokesman for the complex are encouraged that the corporate and administrative change now being worked out will prove to be the turning point of the sometimes troubled complex." Five weeks later under a headline proclaiming "Major changes at the top may help Place Bonaventure," the Post stated that the Concordia Group has been fired by Great West Life Assurance Co., who had hired Trizec to replace them. A year later while Concordia was looking for financial backers for Cité Concordia, the President of the Montreal Trust Co., Frank E. Chase, stated, during a Post interview, in reference to Place Bonaventure that, "you can be sure we're not getting into any more of those deals."

Following this fiasco, the Concordia Group, all of whom are Montreal-based entrepreneurs, established their American credentials by successfully completing a contract for Project Management Services for a $115 million Crown Center development, owned by Hallmark Cards, in Kansas City. Meanwhile, back at the ranch, the group became involved in an $18 million 27-storey office building in Hull, Place du Portage. Little is known about this project save the fact that it only got as far as a large hole in the ground in the middle of Hull. Finally the Federal government stepped in and it is understood with substantial profits to the original developers, completed the project.

At a June 23, 1970 press conference, the Concordia Group announced its full plans for the Cité Concordia project. At this time, it was made quite evident that Concordia had only partial financing, from both the Great West Life Assurance Co., and the Ford Foundation of New York. This financing consisted of a $12,613,901.24 four-year loan, due June 1, 1972, at seven and a half per cent from the G.W.L.A. Co., and a more complicated $10,800,000 loan (principally in promissory notes payable on demand) from the Ford Foundation. It is uncertain how much of the Ford money has been cashed, however if it all has, it will come due in December. At the end of March of this year, representatives from both firms stated that Concordia was behind in its interest payments.

In order to complete phase one, an estimated seventy million dollars is needed. This kind of money Concordia dimply doesn't have. Their poor financial record and adverse publicity (i.e. the aforementioned Case quotation) has resulted in it being extremely difficult for Concordia to raise the needed capital.

Another indication of the poor fiscal position of Concordia is that they are behind in their municipal taxes $108,409.52. Although it is not uncommon for development companies not to pay their municipal taxes, because the interest rate on back taxes is lower than the market rate for real estate development capital, the taxes when unpaid serve as a cheap loan. It is however interesting to note that the property taxes that are due are for the houses in phase 2 and 3. In other words, at present none of the rent money from the occupied Concordia houses in the area is going to pay the taxes. Presumably, Concordia has other more pressing needs, like the $78,000 monthly interest on just the Great West money. On the day demolition started the President of Concordia Estates Ltd., Norman Nerenberg stated on the CBC's Hourglass that Concordia did not have the money to start construction once demolition was finished.

What will happen is of course still up in the air. There are rumours to the effect that the Sheraton Hotel chain is negotiating with Concordia. Nevertheless, it seems unlikely that Concordia will get the complete sum needed for construction. After all, few hotels are worth a $70 million investment. The future is, at best, dark for Concordia on the financial front.

People's Power...Citizens' Plan For Area Renovation

The proposed Cité Concordia Project has forced the Milton-Park Citizens' Committee to confront many serious problems. One of the most pressing of these is the question of a viable alternative which would preserve the character of the community and maintain the low rent housing that exists here.

It was with these aims in mind that the committee and a group of architecture students established a Community Design Workshop at 3476 Park Ave. in September 1971. Similar facilities have also been established in other parts of the city—in Pte. St. Charles, Griffintown and Verdun.

The people involved in the workshop have been working very hard to prepare plans for the renovation of existing housing. They have concentrated their efforts on the block bounded by Hutchison, Park, Milton and Prince Arthur. The priorities in the development of these plans are to renovate houses wherever possible and to incorporate into the plans adequate outdoor recreational spaces, parking facilities, etc. Three alternate plans have been prepared. The first of these would involve renovation of all existing housing. The second and third involve demolition of some of the buildings in the poorest condition and construction of new buildings. These new buildings would preserve the character of the existing housing. The final choices on what plans would be implemented would be based on the priorities expressed by the community, financial resources available, and the extent of government participation.

In conjunction with these plans the Milton-Park Citizens' Committee has presented a proposal to the city asking that renovation and management of the closed houses be placed under the control of a non-profit community housing corporation, to be funded by a government loan. The corporation would give a real measure of control to tenants.

With the help of an Opportunities for Youth grant the workshop is continuing its operations through the summer. The group is working on plans to build a park in the backyard of the University Settlement and studies are being done on other spots in the area which could be transformed into small parks and information centres.

To date there has been very little community participation in the activities of the workshop and few people even know about it. So, drop around to the workshop at 3476 Park Ave., no. 5 to see and discuss the plans.

On Housing

First appeared in OUR GENERATION
Vol. 13, No. 1, Winter 1979

Lucia Kowaluk

WHEN PEOPLE OWN and/or control their own housing and when they do their own labour, they enjoy it more, take better care of it, the urban environment in which it is placed improves, and it is more economical from every point of view.

This essential truth appears to be valid whether the land on which the home stands is owned by the resident, by a co-operative, or by the State. It is important for socialists to understand this because the goals of unalienated labour, of control of one's environment and of the common good appear to be as much at work with regard to small private ownership of one's home as they are with one or another form of co-operative or community ownership—the ultimate goal of most socialists.

This poses a dilemma which socialists have not yet answered. On the one hand, lauding small private ownership of land—"The American Dream"—represents all the forces of reaction in North American society. The literature of socialist thought is full of detailed criticism of this position, and there is no need to repeat it here. On the other hand, the unhappy direction of our own capitalist society as well as the state-run economies of the communist-bloc countries toward greater and greater centralization of land ownership, both by capitalist developers and by state-run bureaucracies, is also clear.

Faced with both their rejection of capitalist ownership and control of land and housing as a commodity, and their growing realization that the state bureaucratic control of housing in the so-called "socialist" countries has gone from the frying pan into the fire, libertarian socialists are finding themselves rejecting control from both sides.

In addition to this, the traditional social democratic solution within capitalist societies has also been to rely totally on the State to counter the forces of capitalist might, and we see the results in our own "public" housing, or the municipally-run Council Housing of Great Britain that Colin Ward condemns.

Faced with these failures, and continuing to search for property relationships which will allow people the best housing a society can offer, socialists would do well to look again at the privately owned and personally cared-for housing of the "other economy" (so called because the financing of the housing and the labour involved all operate outside the regular professional economy of our society), described by McGill professor Roger Krohn, as a means to attain this—at least for the present, within our system which does not seem to be withering away, nor is about to be eliminated.

Krohn's book, *The Other Economy: The Internal Logic of Local Rental Housing* (1977), co-authored by two of his students, contains the research of six of his graduate students from the McGill department of sociology. The book describes research concerning housing in six inner-city Montreal neighbourhoods. The research set out simply to investigate tenant-landlord relationships in a variety of neighbourhoods, but found a collection of data that revealed a common-sense conclusion: where housing is lived in by the owner—who may rent out additional flats in the same piece of property, who does much of the work on the property himself, and who does not count his labour as cost on an accounting sheet—the housing turns out to be well-kept, attractive, stable or upgrading to neighbourhoods; it attracts long-term tenancy who have the same attitude as the landlord; and it is cheap to live in, both for the tenants and the residents. Krohn found no class division for this fact; it was true regardless of the social class of the tenants and owners.

For a Montrealer, this book is especially fun to read. Historical neighbourhood tidbits are interspersed with descriptions of familiar streets and incidents. For example, the upgrading of St. Dominique, Coloniale, de Bullion, and Hôtel-de-Ville Streets north of Sherbrooke, and especially north of Prince Arthur, which is obvious to any Montrealer who has walked in the area, is now explained, *not* as the result of any urban renewal scheme (courtesy of tax-spending, controlling governments), but as a result of the efforts of modest Portuguese immigrants who pooled their resources and labour with friends and relatives; bought first one dilapidated house, then another; and fixed them while living in them—everyone working on one, and then the next—without having to borrow money at commercial rates, to hire workmen at commercial rates, nor to get involved in federal "helping" schemes. The results have been good housing, attained with little expenditures of capital, and pride in and control of one's environment. The essential elements in this scheme are the proprietorship of the housing, and the personal non-commercial labour involved in the renovation and upkeep.

In studying a very slowly deteriorating neighbourhood (Eastern Outremont), Krohn's students found that housing that had been stable for up to thirty years, and remained so at the time of the study, was housing of resident-owners who did a lot of their own work, and which attracted stable tenants—many of whom stayed in the same house for 20 to 30 years—who themselves did a lot of their own work in return for stable (and low) rents. Both tenants and landlords were held together by an unwritten, mutually beneficial code. It is easy to imagine how this arrangement of sharing and mutual respect results in good, cheap housing which benefits both the residents and the neighbourhood.

The slow deterioration of the neighbourhood began as property was bought up by absentee landlords—in particular, speculators who cared neither for good housing nor stable, attractive neighbourhoods. And here is where capitalism rears its ugliest and most destructive head. Krohn's studies found that when land, whether privately, co-operatively or publicly owned, is valued *primarily* for its use value, everyone benefits. When its use value is disregarded, and its primary value becomes that of a profit-making commodity, everyone loses—in the short run, the users, and, in the long run, society as a whole, even the speculator (who must occasionally come into the deteriorated, ugly, and dangerous city form his safe suburban enclave).

The remaining studies of Krohn's book are variations of the same themes with different examples and nuances. His conclusion is clear, and all the more interesting because the author did not set out to prove it. Indeed, he did not even begin with it as an undeveloped idea. Rather, it emerged from the data. A very interesting and valuable book!

Colin Ward's book *Housing: An Anarchist Approach* (1976) is a collection of essays and speeches, written by him, and published elsewhere over a period of twenty years. Housing questions in the UK are the primary issue, but other issues—the professional role of planners and architects, public housing (how it evolves and how tenants feel about it), to name a few—are also dealt with.

The subtitle of the book—"An Anarchist Approach"—is reflected throughout in the simple notion, already expressed in Krohn's book, that people like to own and control their housing without either a landlord or the State telling them what they can and cannot do. Because the book is offering a critique, largely of British government housing policy, Council Housing ("public housing," in our country), and various ministries, Ward is criticizing the State more than capitalism. However, there are enough references to the latter to make it clear to the reader that, as expressions of authoritarian control, the two can be lumped together.

For Ward, the squatter's movements in various Third World countries offer a better solution for poor people's housing needs than the Council Housing in Britain. He devotes one section of the book to describing this phenomenon. We know that one of the most powerful people's movements in Chile, during Allende's regime (see *Our Generation*, Sullivan, vol. 10, no. 1), was the housing co-operative movement with old squatter's traditions. Ward quotes extensively from John Turner, a British architect and anarchist with years of observation and work in Latin American.

The squatter barriada-builder who chooses to invest his life's savings in an environment that he creates, forms himself in the process. The person, as the member of a family and of a local community, finds in the responsibilities and activities of home-building and local improvement the creative dialogue essential for self-discovery and growth. Because the poor are the majority in Lima and because the government controls neither the material nor the human resources necessary for the satisfaction of essential housing needs, the poor must act for themselves—and if the official rules and regulations get in the way, these, along with any policemen who may be sent in to enforce them, are generally swept aside. (p. 78-9)

In another section of the book, Colin Ward describes alternatives to the present English Council housing. He mentions the current activity in New York City of "urban homesteading," set out in a booklet called the Urban Homesteading Assistance Board or UHAB, which describes a particular set of housing projects, sponsored by the Cathedral of St. John the Divine in New York City.

With the help of the paid staff, the UHAB project uses government money, at 1% interest, to take over and renovate abandoned buildings in New York City—spending relatively little money because much of the labour is done by the prospective tenants, making the final rents half of what they would be using professional labour. In this way, the term "sweat equity" is used to describe this process.

A unique feature of this New York City project is that the abandoned buildings are legally abandoned, as well as left empty. That is, the owner relinquishes all title to them, refusing to pay taxes on them or to be responsible for them. This phenomenon has become fairly well known and is the result, the landlords claim, of their inability through rent control to raise rents enough to pay for repairs and profits. The abandoned buildings are then expropriated by the City of New York and sold for $1 to a Homesteading Project.

The possibilities of co-operative ownership (these are all large, four and five-storey walk-ups, so the possibility of a single, low-income owner is eliminated) and control that this abandonment offers is exciting. The values expounded in both Krohn's and Ward's books are made possible here. A crucial question, however, is the degree to which the State, both the federal and city, still controls the housing and tenants. In other words, if the homesteading housing, "sold" to tenants for $1, really changes hands, giving the tenants complete control, the prospect is exciting. If the State retains residual control, we have simply a new form of public (or Council) housing.

In Canada, we know the happy results of the federal government's "gifts" to housing. The Dennis-Fish Report of 1972 (*Programs in Search of a Policy*, by Michael Dennis and Susan Fish, 1972) exposed the CMHC for what it is: namely, the federal government's intervention in the housing and construction market, in such a way as to be most helpful to developers. The fact that thousands of Canadians now own their own expensive, commercially-built, suburban homes, thanks to CMHC programs and subsidies, does not deny the fact that CMHC's goal is to fuel the private developer-controlled market. Recent proposed changes in the law, announced in the spring of 1978, which would have had the net result of tightening bureaucratic control of housing co-operatives, have been scathingly denounced by the Co-operative Housing Foundation of Canada (237 Metcalfe St., Ottawa).

A Proposal

Land is wealth and so is housing. So, as long as it remains thus, and is not valued for its use alone, it will be controlled to increase in value as wealth rather than as use. Good inner-city housing at low rents cannot be a profit-making commodity in our present market system. If the fact is not already obvious, Roger Krohn's research has made that clear. We can have luxury city-housing or new suburban housing built by a developer, if we want to pay for all the labour and profits or have it subsidized by our taxes, or we can make our own housing. But, it cannot be good and cheap and be part of the market system. The more often commodities are removed from the profit-making spheres, as in co-operatives, and valued for their use value alone, the better deal will be available for the average consumer. But only when the housing thus attained *remains* valued for its use and does not become a commodity to be sold for profit will the housing continue to stay cheap and good. Once it enters the commodity market, it will be worth more than the labour and materials that went into it.

This is why there is a substantial moral distinction between owning a house in order to retain its use value and owning a house in order to sell it for profit, notwithstanding its individual or co-operative status.

Ensuring that housing retains a use value, rather than a commodity value, is impossible in a capitalist society. The thrust of capitalism is always to accumulate wealth for its own sake and not for its use. What this means for housing is that there will always be pressure on small owners to sell to big owners, and in the process, the small owner will lose the freedom and economy he had. The search for a blueprint Utopia to prevent this from happening has always driven reformers, although it eludes us still. Rather, what seems a more possible approach is to strive to realize, as much as possible, certain basic principles, and to implement them, here and now, in small ways.

Colin Ward points out very basic principles which should be kept in mind: most people love the process of slowly improving their domicile, and *no one* likes to be bossed and controlled beyond that which his elementary sense of community tells him is necessary.

So, keeping these in mind, let us try to present a scenario which could be part of the housing policy of a reform city government—using, as a case in point, Montreal, where abandoned housing is not legally abandoned as in New York City, but is boarded up and not used.

Abandoned housing is a scourge of most modern cities. Land speculation and the use of housing for profit have made it advantageous for landlords to board up buildings, rather than provide decent housing. It is, nevertheless, a phenomenon that repulses most citizens who are not in the land speculation business.

It is, therefore, elementary that in the short run, before major changes such as some sort of community ownership of all urban land come about, the abandonment of housing not have the protection of the law. Rather than a reform city government giving itself the power to intervene, that government should simply let it be known that it will not give legal protection to housing in an abandoned state.

Any building that could be used for housing and has been abandoned for more than three months would be eligible to be taken over. It should not be expropriated by the city government, but instead would transfer immediately to the tenant who moves in. A number of conditions would have to be laid down to prevent those not in need from simply grabbing first, and to ensure that elementary health and safety regulations be followed.

1. First choice for the tenants would come from the public housing waiting lists; and after that present tenants in public housing. People interested in the prospect of taking over an abandoned house would have to join the waiting list. Obviously, not everyone on the list would choose to take over an abandoned house because of the work and expense involved.
2. An outright, immediate, no-questions-asked government grant of $5,000 would be given to enable the immediate maintenance of health and fire standards. The tenant would have to meet the building code regulations of any private owner, but beyond that he would have complete control of the money.
3. After that, he is on his own. Like any private owner, he would assume the responsibility for taxes and upkeep. Krohn's book is full of examples of ways in which the poorest people managed to improve their housing when they felt that they would benefit.

    The problem of helping those families who have no resources with which to fix up a home is traditionally dealt with by more government handouts. This is done with the best intentions and good will in the world, but a re-examination of the facts pushes us to believe in the resources of even the poorest people. One of Krohn's studies describes an example (used in another context) in which a family on welfare made, by using their own labour and scrounging for materials, so many improvements in their slum home that the landlord raised the rent and they were forced to move (this was in the days before the Rental Board was as widely used as it is today).

Furthermore, every family, regardless of income, budgets a certain amount of money for rent. By squatting in an abandoned house at no cost, that rent money is freed for improvements.

4. He cannot, however, sell the property, house, or land. He can pass it on to his family or anyone else to whom he wants to make a gift. But if he wants to leave the property entirely, it would revert back to the City who would run it as public housing. The tenant's compensation for his time and expense is the privilege of living in the house as an owner for as long as he wants.
5. If the house has more than one living unit (a duplex or triplex, for example), it could be taken over by a legally formed co-operative. If one tenant wants to take the time and expense to bring it all up to standard in order to rent part of it, he could have the privilege and responsibility of doing so as long as he continues to live in one unit, and as long as the rented property meets the housing code. What one owner is able to do with his own labour will never enable him to make a substantial profit.

Socialists may object to this fostering of "petty bourgeois values." An anarchist like Colin Ward writes, however, in answer to the question that the tenant takeover presupposes and exalts the virtues of ownership, that in a desirable social order private ownership of real property would not exist.

> I agree. I agree too that householders, whether owners paying back mortgage loans or tenants, the greater part of whose rent goes in interest payments, are both victims of our economic system. I believe in social ownership of social assets, but I think it is a mistake to confuse society with the state. Co-operative ownership seems to me to be a better concept of social ownership than ownership by the state or the municipality. But in the pragmatic terms since we have reached a point where the majority of dwellings are owner-occupied, I want to extend the benefits that accrue to the owner-occupied to the tenant. (p. 156)

In addition, this proposal has an essential non-capitalist principle: it does not allow an accumulation of wealth beyond its use value. It does not make a commodity out of housing. This is the essential principle socialists must struggle for: to retain the use value and control by the user of what we use, and not turn such items into commodities.

REFERENCES

Krohn, Roger G., Berkeley Fleming, and Marilyn Manzer. 1977. *The Other Economy: The Internal Logic of Local Rental Housing*. Canadian Experience Series. Toronto: P. Martin Associates.

UHAB (The Urban Homesteading Assistance Board). 1977. *Third Annual Progress Report*. New York: Cathedral House, 1047 Amsterdam Avenue.

Ward, Colin. 1976. *Housing: An Anarchist Approach*. London: Freedom Press.

Lucia Kowaluk
Montreal, January 1979

Arrests and Trial
The Review
Friday, January 26, 1973

Concordia Salut!

The upcoming trial of the "Milton Park 26" marks the latest stage of the fight of the Milton Park Citizens' Committee (MPCC) to "stop Concordia."

The MPCC was founded five years ago to oppose Cité Concordia, the high-rise development scheme that Concordia Investments Ltd. had planned, in the name of progress, for the Milton Park area. Members of the committee thoroughly canvassed the residents of the area and found the great majority to be against Concordia. Earliest members of the Committee considered Cité Concordia to be basically an oversight of the politicians and bureaucrats who, once informed of the real facts, would set the matter straight. This was not the case—and so a process of self-education began.

As McGill English professor, David Williams, one of the founding members of the MPCC, pointed out recently, early encounters with city government officials radically changed MPCC's understanding of the situation.

"First of all, they knew exactly what was going on. Second, they agreed with us that Cité Concordia was undesirable for all the reasons we gave. Yet, in spite of that, they admitted that they were going to do all they could to ensure its success."

Obviously there was no simple oversight involved! Equally obvious was that the elected representatives of the people simply did not respond to the expressed needs or desires of the people. What they responded to was, as some of the members put it, the needs of the market. For David Williams, among others, Cité Concordia gradually changed from an oversight to an indication of the actual workings of power in our society. Fighting Concordia took on more and more the aspect of fighting the "system," even though this was seldom made explicit.

During the next three years, the situation was more or less at a stalemate. Concordia was able to convince and cajole the tenants of houses in the first phase of the plan to vacate the 255 units in question, but were unable to raise the funds for demolition and construction. The Committee dogged their footsteps, making potential investors and sponsors wary.

During this time, Cité Concordia received the full support of the Drapeau administration and the Provincial government, with at least two bills being passed in Quebec at Concordia's request.

Nevertheless, there was cautious optimism among the committee members. Numerous community, labour, professional, and other groups endorsed the demands of the Committee and it appeared that, notwithstanding the role of the government, Cité Concordia was doomed.

The basically optimistic mood of the group was reflected in the work of the Community Design Workshop. Staffed by fifth-year students in the McGill School of Architecture, the CDW provided the Committee with alternative architectural and financial plans for the area; plans intent on preserving and renovating the existing houses—especially the 255 that had been closed for almost three years, and had begun to deteriorate. The various levels of government ignored the alternate plans (though government experts frequently praised their design), either claiming housing to be outside their constitutional jurisdiction or pointing out that the government had no right interfering in "free enterprise."

By winter of 1972, the membership of the Committee had changed somewhat, having gained several younger and perhaps more impatient members. The sight of 255 houses rotting away became generally intolerable and a series of letters, petitions, meetings with city officials, etc. were arranged. When these failed, peaceful demonstrations were organized to draw popular attention to the deteriorating houses, at a time when low-income housing was so desperately needed. Still no action from the city!

By spring of that year the MPCC decided that the issue could wait no longer. Park Avenue, which had been the hub of the community, with many interesting stores and shops, looked like the main street of a ghost town. A symbolic occupation of one of the closed houses was planned. A day before the planned occupation, Concordia began to demolish the building, its president, Norman Nerenberg, admitting that the corporation did not have the money to begin construction.

The rest, as they say, is history (see other articles herein). The Milton Park Committee still meets regularly and the struggle against Concordia continues. But the lessons of spring and summer have made the struggle part of a far wider one. The lessons that were implicitly learned in the early days were explicitly repeated on the streets, in the cells, and before the courts.

If fighting Concordia had in principle meant fighting the "system" it now meant it in practice. Courts, police, and the media had teamed up with Concordia and the two levels of government to screw the citizens.

During the summer, a subcommittee met regularly, trying to analyze and draft a statement of policy on the future orientation of the MPCC. This document was presented in the early fall, thoroughly discussed, and in October, was adopted by the Committee as a general statement of its principles and goals. There was alternative to a capitalist system that produces Cité Concordia. The statement reads in part:

Thousands of signatures on petitions, court injunctions, a hunger strike, detailed alternate plans for the houses, etc., were not about to move Concordia or its supporters. When confronted by direct nonviolent action of the citizens, the response was brutally followed by harassment while the media (especially the English) kept silent. We had confronted a clear case of power: Them that has—gets. In this it was Concordia—representing private property and profit—with all the power, while the citizens were powerless. What matters is power and property!

This is proletarianization: the understanding that one is fundamentally opposed to the interests of that small class of people who have power and those who serve them; that one's long-term goals are therefore directly linked to the needs of the powerless and oppressed.

An inescapable conclusion, it seems to us, follows; we must replace the prevailing capitalist system with one where social and economic decisions and policies are made on the basis of human need and the interests of the great majority. Such a system is called socialism. Socialism cannot be imposed by a small group, it must come to fruition through popular action and popular participation must be maintained as a basic element in any socialist system.

A communitarian spirit has existed in the MPCC for a long time and it must be maintained, just as it must be placed in a wider context. We cannot establish real community control under the prevailing capitalist system—it must be understood as an integral element in pursuing the goal of the establishment of socialism in our society. This requires far more than the actions of a group of people in one neighbourhood. It requires a mass movement of groups working together.

To hope for a transformation of this society, we must set our goals and activities in light of a societal movement that integrates the large majority of the population towards a collective vision of a new social and economic system. The inescapable fact which such an orientation must have, is in the reality of Quebec, and the movement that has arisen within it. To meet the needs of the people of our community means to work for socialism. And this, concretely, means identifying ourselves directly with these popular forces of liberation in Quebec society which can unify workers and citizens' groups. To those who share these goals, the MPCC asks you to join us. Help us and find out more by attending the trial, contribute to the defence funds, and join us at our weekly Tuesday night meetings.

The Trial

On Monday, January 29th, eight people from the Milton Park Citizens' Committee will go on trial at the "Palais de Justice." They are the first of a group of 26 people facing charges of "private mischief" stemming from the May 26th occupation of the rental offices of Concordia Estates Ltd. on Park Avenue.

The action of last May was one of the high points in the five-year struggle of the committee to prevent the demolition of six square blocks of low- and medium-rent housing in "le Quartier Ste. Famille," which is just east of McGill and is commonly known as the student ghetto. On the eve of a planned symbolic long-term "squat-in" in a number of houses that had been closed for a period of two years, Concordia announced that demolition was beginning. At the same time they admitted that they had not yet obtained the necessary financing for the project. Faced with this situation, a number of people occupied one of the houses that was being demolished and held it over the weekend. It was a time of animated conversations on the street and a rapid swelling of the occupation force. However, Tuesday morning saw the appearance of the riot squad. They were met by a "human chain" of close to 100 people on the sidewalk protecting the occupiers. The police cleared the street and removed the occupiers without incident.

Despite prior assurances from the Drapeau regime that demolition would not be allowed before the project had been financed, the city did nothing and demolition continued throughout the week. On the following Friday the occupation of Concordia's offices took place. Demonstrators outside the building were gradually surrounded by a ring of police and after a period of time everyone was arrested. Charges of assault were laid against 59 people who had participated in the occupation.

These and subsequent actions failed to prevent the continuation of demolition. Today one-third of the six block area is an open field. An occasional rat can be seen running between piles of rubble. Recently Concordia announced that an American hotel chain has agreed to finance a hotel in the area.

Nevertheless, the members of the committee still maintain their optimism. They are quietly preparing a campaign to prevent the second phase of Cité Concordia, which calls for further demolition. However, the major focus of action at the present time is the trial.

At the first court appearance, charges were changed from assault to private mischief. This is a more serious charge involving a jury trial and a maximum sentence of 5 years in jail. It also meant that the 11 immigrants who had been charged would be "subject to automatic deportation" except for the possibility of appeal to the Minister of Immigration. Negotiations resulted in the dropping of charges against 10 of these immigrants in return for guilty pleas on the part of a sufficient number of the 59. As a result those who pleaded guilty were placed on probation for one year, after which all records will be cancelled under the provisions of the new leniency law, providing that they "keep the peace" during this period. Charges were not dropped against one immigrant, who still faces possible deportation.

The eight people who go on trial Monday requested that the trial be held in French. The committee feels that due to the selection process a French jury is more likely to be composed of tenants and working people in general. The committee also feels that this is an important expression of support on the part of a mainly English group for the struggle of the Québecois to make French the working language of Quebec. The presiding judge first refused to grant the defendants a trial in the language of their choice, but this decision has now been reserved until the opening of the trial itself.

The defense will be conducted, not only on strictly legal grounds, but will also provide evidence to justify the actions which led to the charges. The defendants will attempt to show that their actions were correct and necessary under the circumstances.

It should be a political trial of some interest!

McGill Daily
Vol. 62, No. 74. Thursday, February 8, 1973

MPCC Members Acquitted
by Celemenski Klinkholl Thompson
Seven members of the Milton-Park Citizens' Committee (MPCC) were acquitted yesterday of the charges of private mischief.

The trial, which arose out of the May 26 occupation of the offices of Concordia Estates Limited, was marked by extensive discussions of the wider issues involved and not simply the legal aspects. Much of the defense's testimony concerned the profit oriented nature of Concordia, the bad faith in which they had acted throughout their contact with the Milton-Park Citizens' Committee, the housing problem in Montreal, and the rights of citizens to determine what happens to their community. In addition the defense attempted to prove that the occupiers had just cause to be at the Concordia offices since they were there to obtain and relay information and that they had not impaired the normal business affairs of Concordia.

On Tuesday, the defense called Philip Coleman, a founder and ex-president of Concordia from 1959 to 1967. Most of his testimony concerned Cité Concordia, the project Concordia is planning to build on the land which they have cleared by the demolition of homes and other buildings in the area. He testified that:
- Concordia as early as 1968 had difficulty obtaining money to purchase the houses in the area;
- Cité Concordia, in his opinion, was not economically viable;
- The housing in the project would in no way be available to the average working man (for economic reasons).

Finally, when asked for what purposes Concordia undertook the project, Coleman replied in one word—"profit."

McGill English professor David Williams described the difficulties of negotiations between MPCC and Concordia and their eventual breakdown due to Concordia's refusal to meet with MPCC. He also said that John Lynch-Staunton, vice-president of the Executive Committee of Montreal City Council, had assured MPCC that there would be no demolition until Concordia could prove that they were ready, and had the funds, to begin construction (something which they have been unable to do). He further testified that he himself had not heard the order to disperse and that it was difficult to hear due to the noise caused by construction in the area. In addition, he substantiated the earlier testimony of Ed Smith, Executive Director of the University Settlement, that a member of MPCC was not allowed to leave the area after the order to disperse was read, and was subsequently arrested.

Yesterday, the court heard the summations of both the prosecution and the defense, as well as the judge's charging of the jury, before the not guilty verdict was returned. Michel Leclair, the defense attorney, began his comments by asking the jurors to consider which party in the conflict had brought more harm to the society—the citizens who struggled to preserve their community, or the corporation who destroyed the community in order to build high-rises and make profit.

He then stated that the prosecution had not proved beyond reasonable doubt that any of the accusations were true and that, in fact, the prosecution witnesses had contradicted themselves in several instances. He also stressed that the citizens had just cause to be at the offices since their purpose was to meet with Mr. Nerenberg, president of Concordia. He went on to say that the offices were specifically used for tenants' business and complaints.

Citizens, he continued, had an obligation to protect themselves. Recent actions, such as the Cabano struggle, had demonstrated, given frustration by due process, the only effective means to achieve on their own behalves.

He countered the prosecution's attempts to discredit Claire Culhane's motives through its allegations that she was a "professional agitator." He said that her participation in the cause of the Vietnamese people by working in a hospital in Vietnam, by writing a book, condemning Canada's involvement in Vietnam, and by demonstrating arose from her humanist convictions. In the case of the actions of the MPCC, she participated because of these convictions and the fact that she had been hired as a community organizer to help the people of the community articulate their demands.

Similarly the other defendants had earlier stated the motives which resulted in their own participation. These motives were basically to preserve their community in the face of its destruction.

The jury returned the verdict after an hour and a half of deliberation. It is likely that as a result of this verdict the charges against the remaining 19 individuals arrested at the same time will be dropped.

Housing Co-ops:
Citizen Control or Social Service

Josh Hawley

> *"The early efforts of poor people to improve their own housing conditions failed to expand for lack of capital. Investors, then as now, found easier ways to get rich than by financing working-class housing. This is where the Victorian philanthropists moved in, satisfied with a 'modest return' on their capital."*
> —Colin Ward, *Tenants Take Over* (1974)

THE OWENITES and the Rochdale Pioneers, those early-nineteenth century British co-operators, inspired a worldwide movement. Ironically, as Colin Ward wrote decades ago, while the movement strengthened in other European countries, the British co-op movement never shook its early reliance on charity and philanthropy. Co-op housing in Sweden, for example, "depended strongly on the initiative of tenants; it did not, as in the United Kingdom, become the instrument of liberal employers and philanthropists making provision for what were referred to as the 'working classes.'"[1]

In the Milton-Parc neighbourhood of Montreal, where working class people organized heavily for years to defend their homes and improve their living conditions through resident-control of housing and land, it was ultimately a wealthy philanthropist who stepped in. Phyllis Lambert, of the Bronfman dynasty, and her organization, Heritage Montreal, helped Milton-Parc residents enormously by putting heavy pressure on the government and business people to save the Milton-Parc buildings for heritage reasons, but only with the guarantee of citizen control. Similarly, it was a "wealthy Montreal pawnbroker and real estate bargain-hunter,"[2] Harry Mendelsohn, who bought the properties from the developer for $4.5 million, and, for reasons still unclear to this day,[3] kept the properties off the market until Canada Mortgage and Housing Corporation (CMHC), the federal government's housing agency, purchased them for $5.5 million—a modest return on his investment. With the Milton-Parc properties securely in public hands, the residents spent the next few years organizing into housing co-ops and figuring out how to permanently remove their neighbourhood from the market and abolish speculation.

The Milton-Parc co-ops were created through the efforts and the initiative of neighbourhood residents, facilitated by wealthy philanthropists, and financed and

Table 1: Average number of units per housing co-op by region			
Region	Number of Co-ops	Number of Units	Average Number of Units per Co-op
British Columbia	275	15,784	57
Prairies	129	6,734	52
Ontario	551	44,181	80
Quebec	1,130	22,501	20
Atlantic Provinces	122	3,164	26
Yukon, NWT and Nunavut	5	162	32
Total	2,212	92,526	42

evaluated by the state. It was created as a social service—to provide housing to people with very low incomes, low incomes and low-middle incomes—and is entirely owned and controlled by its residents. Unfortunately, the Milton-Parc project is unique among social housing and housing co-ops in Canada.

This chapter explores how in Canada, mirroring the British mode of housing co-op development, the co-op movement has come to be marked by the top-down approach of housing professionals and the government, facilitated by a national co-op housing lobby group.

An Overview of Co-op Housing In Canada

Co-op housing in Canada is large: about 250,000[4] people live in 2,212 incorporated co-ops across the country (see Table 1).[5] Housing co-ops that receive or have received financial subsidies from the federal or provincial governments fall under the social housing portfolio[6] of CMHC. Co-ops account for 15% of this portfolio, which in total comprises over 613,500 social housing units across the country.[7]

Within this one specific form of tenure, there are a variety of typologies. Co-ops can be new builds or conversions; they can be multi-floor houses or studio apartments in a high-rise; and they can be made up of a few friends or thousands of strangers. This variation is amplified when comparing regions. The two most populous provinces, Ontario and Quebec, each occupy one end of what can be called the "scale of co-op housing centralization" (see Table 2).

Ontario has 551 housing co-ops, with an average of 80 units per co-op. Quebec, at the other end of the scale, has over twice as many co-ops but less than half as many units, with an average of only 20 units per co-op. These two provinces, which account for 61.5% of the entire population of Canada, account for 72% of the total number of co-op units across the country.

Table 2: Average rate of membership in CHFC by region		
Region	Number of CHF Canada Members	Membership Rate %
British Columbia	197	71.64
Prairies	82	63.57
Ontario	508	92.20
Quebec	N/A	N/A
Atlantic Provinces	110	90.16
Yukon, NWT and Nunavut	5	100
Total	902	83.51

Finally, 92% of co-ops in Ontario belong to the Co-operative Housing Federation of Canada (CHFC), the sector's national lobby group. According to CHFC, no individual housing co-ops in Quebec belong directly to CHFC; instead they may be affiliated through their regional associations' membership in CHFC. For example, if a co-op in Montreal is a member of the Fédération des Coopératives d'Habitation Intermunicipale du Montréal Métropolitain (FECHIMM), it is indirectly a member of CHFC, because FECHIMM is a member of CHFC.

These statistics raise a number of questions: How did co-op housing come to occupy such a substantial part of Canada's social housing landscape? Why is there such a large difference in the size of co-ops between the two largest provinces? How did this form of tenure become known as "co-operative housing" in the first place? What are the factors that have allowed the current state of co-op housing to emerge? How has the movement developed?

To try and find some answers, it is useful to turn to the historical record.

Co-operation Is Life

There is a difficulty in defining a movement around a universal, "automatic"[8] operation such as co-operation. Therefore, I will only very briefly consider co-operation on a metaphysical level. This also involves acknowledging that this chapter does not attempt to challenge to the Western monopolization of co-operation.

Karl Marx wrote in *Capital Volume I* that the power that "excites emulation between individuals and raises their animal spirits…is due to co-operation itself. When the labourer co-operates systematically with others, he strips off the fetters of his individuality, and develops the capabilities of his species."[9] Echoing this elemental statement, Peter Kropotkin, in *Mutual Aid*, gave strong evidence that co-operation should be seen as a driving force of life and "a law of Nature and a factor of evolution" rather than "to admit a pitiless inner war for life within each species, and to see in that war a condition of progress."[10]

Co-operation as a way of being and living together has existed on Turtle Island well before Europeans introduced it as a movement. Whichever "father of co-operation" is iconized, the reality is that co-operation cannot be reduced to a social movement, which by definition is a reaction, an "attempt to bring about or resist change…or to create an entirely new order."[11] The co-op movement "was essentially a reaction to the economic and social problems confronting urban workers and small farmers."[12]

Rather, co-operation, like utopia, is immanent.[13] It is found in the "account-ability to the people…life as a community, the achievement of consensual decision making and participation in all levels of political processes…and in the questions concerning self, peoplehood, and nationhood…clustered around the issue of membership in the community" of Kahnawà:ke.[14] It is also found in "the Nishnaabeg systems…including story or theory, language learning, ceremony, hunting, fishing, ricing, sugar making, medicine making, politics, and governance."[15] It is immanent because, according to Leanne Betasamosake Simpson's account of Nishnaabewin, "*how* we live, *how* we organize, *how* we engage in the world—the process—not only frames the outcome, it is the transformation."[16]

The Canadian Voice

The mainstream co-op housing movement in Canada has declared itself to be the "one voice" for housing co-ops across the country. However the discourse around co-op housing in Canada cannot be attributed to one book, one group or one leader. It may emerge through board meetings, federation conferences, and "plain language" educational materials[17], but also appears as much, if not more, through community gardens, encounters in the park, botched subsidy calculations, and eviction notices. It varies between people and over time, but it is carried by every individual who has ever had any experience in a housing co-op. This sentiment is shared by Ian MacPherson, one of this country's most recognized co-operators, who wrote, "The 'movement' has a life beyond institutions, often stretching deeply into cultural, community, kinship, and class relationships. The movement is not easily measured. This is a challenge for historians."[18]

Despite the day-to-day neighbourly interactions, the reality is that mainstream co-op housing is a state-administered sector and thus must be presented as a cohesive body with one voice so it can lobby the government for funding, enabling it to survive.

What is the one voice? A good place to start is with CMHC, which concerns itself solely with incorporated non-profit housing co-ops that have received federal or provincial funding.[19] In its first major housing co-op program evaluation conducted in 1992, CMHC provides a description of the "Structure of the Canadian Co-operative Housing Movement" based on a May 1988 communiqué from CHFC:

> The co-operative housing movement in Canada is multi-tiered. It comprises a national organisation of housing co-operatives, local, regional and provincial organisations which develop new co-operatives and provide services to existing ones, associations of people employed by co-operatives, and housing co-operatives themselves. Members of the national association join directly, or indirectly through membership in another organisation.
>
> In general, the movement is founded on democratic principles, so each member enjoys one vote in the co-operative in which they live.[20]

CMHC recognizes the movement as being definitively structured around CHFC and the regional federations, despite noting that a "number of co-operatives funded under the NHA [National Housing Act] are not affiliated with the Co-operative Housing Federation and operate outside this formal structure."[21] Whatever a co-op's reason for non-affiliation—whether it is actively autonomous or just isolationist—CMHC sees them as separate from the movement.

To an extent, CMHC is correct. In the foreword to the book *Under construction: A History of Co-operative Housing in Canada*,[22] the current executive director of CHFC writes that the story of the lobby—CHFC—is the story of the "movement and *all* [emphasis added] of its voices."[23] Before the federal government got involved with housing co-ops on a national level, CHFC, then called the Co-operative Housing Foundation, was created as the voice of the movement. It was born not from grassroots organizing, but from the top of the broader Canadian co-op and labour movements. Executives from the Co-operative Union of Canada and the Canadian Labour Congress came together in 1968 in the interest of delegating the labour movement's housing concerns to a specialized body.[24] In *Under Construction*, a former executive director of CHFC acknowledges the federation's intent to craft a monolithic voice:

> There is a theory in co-operative housing circles that you don't start with a national organization. In our case proponents of the co-operative movement were convinced that a concerted effort at the national level was needed to promote co-operative housing and to get the government to assist in bringing it about. They created the Co-operative Housing Foundation

when Willow Park was the only continuing housing co-op for families in the country. CHF served as a catalyst for co-operative housing development in Canada and accounts in no small part for the movement's success in growing to its present size.[25]

Since then, CHFC has become extremely effective as a lobby group, often receiving all-party support, and at maintaining its image as the representative voice of not only the movement, but of the hundreds of thousands of residents of co-ops across the country. But with any movement that grows to the size where it becomes removed from the people it claims to represent, let alone with one that was formed from the top, counter voices will struggle to be heard. People inside the sector remain free to draw upon housing co-op discourse and may derive their own meaning and expectations from the movement. Housing co-ops, as an important part of the greater co-op movement and the struggle for housing rights, carry a legacy of political theory and practice and must reckon with how this history has shaped them and to what degree they are accountable to it.

The Movement

The Nature of Co-operation by John G. Craig (1993) provides a detailed genealogy[26] of the co-op movement. More than a linear history of the movement, the book discusses the emergence of a social movement from a condition, that of co-operation, that is present in virtually every theory and form of social organization, including capitalism.[27] Craig writes that the development of co-operation into a *bona fide* social movement, through "contractual" as opposed to informal or "traditional" co-operation,[28] came with certain baggage:

> The emergence of elites and the development of monolithic organizations are of great concern in many egalitarian movements, and they are a source of theoretical problems in the development of a sociology of co-operation... Some radical and aggressive members may seek more change and more purity in form; others may be more conservative and content with the achievements already made or in-progress. The movement may survive such internal conflict, but eventually, having run its course, it will come to an end...The extent of the movement's apparent achievements is often disillusioning to idealists; but in many cases, these individuals may underestimate the progress that has been made.[29]

In *Mutual Aid*, Kropotkin presents a genealogy of the practice of individuals working together for communal benefit, yet he barely touches on co-operation as a movement. What he does write concerns precisely what Craig warned of: that a single-voiced movement creates internal conflict. Kropotkin's analysis of the co-op movement is not very flattering, although he ends on a somewhat optimistic note:

> Co-operation, especially in Britain, is often described as "joint-stock individualism"; and such as it is now, it undoubtedly tends to breed a co-operative egotism, not only towards the community at large, but also among the co-operators themselves. It is, nevertheless, certain that at its origin the movement had an essentially mutual-aid character. Even now, its most ardent promoters are persuaded that co-operation leads mankind to a higher harmonic stage of economic relations, and it is not possible to stay in some of the strongholds of co-operation in the North without realizing that the great number of the rank and file hold the same opinion. Most of them would lose interest in the movement if that faith were gone; and it must be owned that within the last few years broader ideals of general welfare and of the producers' solidarity have begun to be current among the co-operators. There is undoubtedly now a tendency towards establishing better relations between the owners of the co-operative workshops and the workers.[30]

Kropotkin identified the movement grew around one monolithic voice, one which has plagued co-ops since their origins and can be traced back to the cult of personality around the "fathers."

The Utopian Retreat from Politics

Many histories of the co-op movement place its origins in the early nineteenth-century with one utopian thinker in particular: cotton industrialist Robert Owen. Owen is at once called "the father of British Socialism," "the founder of co-operation and secularism" and one of "the fathers of Co-operation."[31] What should become apparent from this section, however, is that Owen "was not the first of the modern Socialist theorists…but one of the last 18th-century rationalists… setting out from New Lanark to claim the Chairmanship of the Board of Directors of the Industrial Revolution."[32] Despite this, Owen's legacy has profoundly shaped the mainstream co-op movement.

Owen's *New View of Society* was built around housing the poor in "Villages of Co-operation"[33] where the workers of his mills would be able to live harmoniously and in healthy communities. Apart from a few examples of isolated British worker co-operatives dating back to the 1760s,[34] the co-op movement started with the question of housing.

However, Owen's co-operative village was not run by the workers themselves. Rather, it was the opposite: the village was a way to control the workers. E.P.

Thompson, in *The Making of the English Working Class* (1963), describes how Owen's perception of workers as unruly shaped his writing and his practice. Workers were in need of education and training so they would become attentive, efficient and orderly. His planned milling societies would essentially act as workhouses, where the poor would live in an environment that would allow them to "become 'useful', 'industrious', 'rational', self-disciplined, and temperate."[35] Owen was a "model paternalist mill-owner and self-made man who canvassed the royalty, courtiers and governments of Europe with his philanthropic proposals."[36] The structure of his villages even echoed Bentham's panopticon by discouraging "immorality...through the introduction of a fining system; and discipline and honesty increased through the setting up of a 'silent monitor', or work-performance indicator, beside each factory-hand."[37] This institutionalized control did not go unnoticed at the time, and a contemporary of Owen, William Cobbett, called the villages "Parallelograms of Paupers."[38] All things considered, Owen's village was simply "an unusually large business unit for the day, requiring a range of management and production-control techniques beyond the needs of the owner of the small mill in a town."[39]

It is ironic that although Owen "was indispensable to the evolution of a working-class consciousness"[40] he, himself, did not hold one. The "notion of working-class advance, by its own self-activity towards its own goals, was alien to Owen even though he was drawn, between 1829 and 1834, into exactly this kind of movement.... Next to 'benevolent' the words most commonly encountered in early Owenite writings are 'provided for them.'"[41] He "reiterated invocations to brotherly love between masters and men" and predicted a "revolution of the human mind directed solely by truth, by charity, and by kindness."[42] His skirting of class antagonisms was more than polite apoliticism—it was consent for the continuation of oppression by the elite. In one example, only two weeks after the Pentrich uprising of 1817, for which the government hanged three insurgents, Owen complimented prime minister Lord Sidmouth's "mild and amiable" disposition.[43]

In the 1820s, Henry Hetherington, a radical publisher and working class organizer, became a follower of Owen's co-operative vision. However, by 1831, he began an open debate, through his weekly newspaper *Poor Man's Guardian*, criticizing Owen's reluctance to engage in substantial political agitation. Owen did not fight to abolish the class system, Heatherington claimed. Instead he looked to the ruling and moneyed elite to improve working class conditions.

> Mr Owen is generally esteemed, and without doubt is, a kind-hearted man—benevolently disposed to do his utmost to better the condition of mankind; but he exhibits a strange perversity of mind in expecting to realise

his political millennium before working men are placed on equal footing with the other classes of the community with regards to political rights...he entertains an absurd idea, that with the aid of a plundering aristocracy, he shall be able to establish Co-operative principles.[44]

By all accounts, Owen was simply naive. But the radicals of his time were unforgiving. They denounced his "comforting system" and his belief in the salvation of patronage. He was mocked for gaining approval from the ruling elite for ideas like co-operation and "Universal Benevolence"[45] which were as old as anything. They joked that these concepts, through Owen's appropriation, were "forced to take refuge and to lie snug for twenty years in the New Lanark mills, with the connivance of the worthy proprietor."[46] Some of his detractors understood co-operative discourse could not be conceived as new[47] nor contained by one monolithic voice:

> Does not Mr. Owen know that the same scheme, the same principles, the same philosophy...of virtue and happiness, were rife in the year 1793, were noised abroad then, were spoken on the house-tops, were whispered in secret, were published in quarto and duodecimo, in political treatises, in plays, poems, songs and romances—made their way to the bar, crept into the church, ascended the rostrum, thinned the classes of the universities... that these "New Views of Society" got into the hearts of poets and the brains of metaphysicians, took possession of the fancies of boys and women, and turned the heads of almost the whole kingdom.[48]

While Owen himself might have been oblivious to the appropriative, panoptical and paternalistic qualities of his villages, the ruling elite certainly wasn't. It saw in Owen's proposals a way to turn the poor into efficient economic contributors while quashing any revolutionary tendencies. Owen was "assisted by numerous, mostly middle-class leaders motivated by religious convictions, general reform sympathies, and fear of more radical movements."[49]

Another figure considered a "father of co-operation" is Charles Fourier. Although celebrated for his contributions to egalitarian thought, notably feminism, his co-op vision shared many of the same characteristics as Owen's.

Fourier's phalansteries—his version of co-operative villages—as described in *The Theory of the Four Movements* (1808/1996), were to be highly communal and ensure absolute equality between men and women. They allowed for private property and were autonomous from state control and subsidy.[50] However, Fourier's utopian communities would not be realized by the poor through any revolutionary means, which would "disturb the established order,"[51] but "from some wealthy philanthropist who might be persuaded to adopt and propagate his system."[52] The phalansteries would not abolish wealth inequality[53] but would instead be mixed-income communities, where "there must be differences of fortune ranging from abject poverty to the possession of 'hundreds of millions.'"[54] With all of this in mind, Fourier might best be described as "the ancestor of all those forms of socialism which seek to combine a minimum of public regulation with a maximum of individual freedom"[55] or, through a more contemporary lens, "an authoritarian communitarian capitalist."[56]

Both Owen and Fourier's proposals and experiments centred around the prerequisite that wealthy philanthropists, when witness to the decrepit conditions of the poor, were to be the initiators of planned, utopian communities. This humanitarian approach was in no small part responsible for associating socialism with philanthropy.[57]

The utopians did not provide "a radical cooperative alternative" and it was not the more recent co-op movement that "renounced political opposition to capitalism, agreed to coexist with capitalism…and adopted free market, commodity social relations—purged of greedy, speculative, exploitive capitalist features—as the basis of cooperation," as Carl Ratner[58] argues. Rather, capitalist and hierarchical features existed in the earliest co-op experiments: "Nineteenth-century advocates of cooperatives, such as Fourier and Owen, were called utopian by their critics not because cooperative business ventures were tenuous nor because cooperatives could not be made to turn a profit; rather, what made them utopian was their retreat from politics and, thus, the whole question of power."[59]

Luckily, Owen and Fourier did not represent the entirety of the early co-op movement, and it is important to identify others who also helped in the early development of the co-op movement.

With the moral justification and cross-class support for co-ops in place, it was only a matter of time before the familiar corporate structure of modern co-ops emerged. The first long-lasting co-op project is attributed to the Rochdale Pioneers. Their goals "were pure Owenism," but their step-by-step method came from "the plan outlined in the 1820s by co-operative leader and theorist Dr. William King of Brighton."[60]

William King, a physician and close friend of Lady Byron—the ex-wife of poet and Baron of Rochdale, Lord Byron—is one character "whose right to be regarded as a father of the modern co-operative movement is indisputable[61] due to the "practical advice given in his magazine *The Co-operator*…[as to] how by opening shops Owen's supporters could use surpluses to save towards their own emancipation."[62] He might be "the most significant" of the early co-op influencers,[63] yet there is very little written about him. What is known is King's co-operativism, like Owen's, was "without the political antagonism towards the upper classes."[64] King's magazine gave practical advice on how to form co-ops, but it was done under the auspices of an elite group that believed it knew what was best for workers: "Dr and Mrs King…and close-knit networks of aristocratic relatives, friends and allies formed the nucleus of an astonishing mixture of Co-operative enthusiasts."[65]

Although the history of the co-op movement has crystallized through certain repeated narratives, recent research[66] suggests the co-op movement might benefit from reorienting itself around the more radical praxes of two other Owenites: William Thompson and Anna Wheeler.

Thompson, whose insight into the expropriation of labour from labourers was quoted by Marx in *Capital*, and Wheeler, a radical feminist, held direct lines of communication with Owen but advocated for a much more political form of co-operation. Thompson "constituted the 'major challenger to Owen's leadership'"[67] and "by 1832 Thompson was preferred over Owen to lead the movement by a majority of the membership…[as] Thompson's co-operative vision was far more democratic than Owen's."[68] Thompson "believed that workers needed to opt out of the competition and ally together to promote their collective interests, since if workers competed against each other they were only sustaining the system that oppresses them."[69]

Thompson and Wheeler, although followers of Owen's vision, believed in a much more class-oriented use-value of co-ops. There was a kernel to the co-op model that could be used by oppressed people for self-determination. How easy it is to activate that kernel is a question that still plays out today.

The Co-op Question: By the State or By the People?

In spite of how hard some of the early proponents of co-ops tried to maintain the movement's apoliticism, to some co-ops represented worker control and class struggle. There has been a lot written about Marx's attitude on co-ops. On the one hand, he believed worker co-ops "are incapable of creating the massive increase in productive capacity that would make socialism and communism possible, and capitalism obsolete."[70] On the other, he saw in them the "potentiality…in working people's abilities to not only run the Parisian factories but the very centers of French political, administrative and military power."[71]

However, if co-ops were indeed to be of use to the working class, it would only be through their mass implementation by the state. Co-ops developing through "the efforts of private workmen," Marx said, were the reason "that plausible noblemen, philanthropic middle-class spouters, and even keen political economists have all at once turned nauseously complimentary to the very co-operative labour system they had vainly tried to nip in the bud."[72] Marx believed co-ops should be structured with "the assistance of the state,"[73] from the national level down: "co-operative labour ought to be developed to national dimensions, and, consequently, to be fostered by national means."[74] This statement, a direct challenge to Proudhonism and anarchism, was made by Marx in his inaugural address to the First International in 1864. "Thus," Robert Graham writes in his account, it was over the co-op question that "the seeds of the conflict in the International between Marx, the Proudhonists, and later, the anarchists, were planted by Marx himself in the *Inaugural Address*."[75]

The co-op question wasn't settled by the First International for either the anarchists or the socialists and over the years co-ops have been, contradictorily, put on pedestals as transformative and shot down as strategies of co-optation. In one example of the former, early anarchist Mikhail Bakunin, writing in 1866, claimed co-ops could spell the end for nations:

> Working men's co-operative associations are a new development in history; we are witnessing their birth at this moment, and can only imagine but not determine the vast expansion they will undoubtedly undergo and the new political and social conditions to which they will give rise. It is possible, indeed highly probably, that eventually…they will provide the whole of human society with a new constitution, no longer divided into nations but into different industrial groupings, and organized according to the requirements not of politics but of production.[76]

In a 1996 lecture to architects, anarchist Colin Ward argued the solution to the problems of the complex bureaucratization associated with modernist residential towers common in North America and Europe "is to develop systems of dweller control through the various forms of housing co-operatives."[77] However, in the 1973 book *Anarchy in Action*, Ward acknowledges how housing co-ops, although examples of "*direct action*,"[78] inevitably get co-opted by the state. He describes the four stages "common to all examples of popular direct action in housing in a non-revolutionary situation," with the final step being to quell any further uprising:

1. Initiation: the individual action or decision that begins the campaign, the spark that starts the blaze;
2. Consolidation: when the movement spreads sufficiently to constitute a threat to property rights and becomes big enough to avoid being snuffed out by the authorities;
3. Success: when the authorities have to concede to the movement what it has won;

4. Official action: usually undertaken unwillingly to placate the popular demand, or to incorporate it in the status quo."[79]

The legislated co-optation and recognition of the poor through the provision of self-managed housing is a form of "strategic 'domestication'"[80] by the state. It aligns itself very well with Owen's "political quietism"[81] and the belief in rationality, order and the "grand design" above everything—including free will.[82]

Yet co-op housing remains ostensibly synonymous with resident-led housing, even while many co-ops now have very low participation among residents.

The complicated history of co-op housing has created multiple focal points to centre justifications for its existence. The first is found in the working class struggle over housing free from the oppression of landlords, private or otherwise. This is the story of co-ops formed from tenants' rights movements and squats in response to discrimination, slum conditions and displacement.[83]

Another is found in groups coming together based on shared identities to create prefigurations of communal living and mutual aid. Although this captures housing co-ops formed from the free-love and drug culture of the 1960s and 1970s, such as the notorious Rochdale College in Toronto,[84] most are not radical and revolve primarily around identity and self-help.

The intersections between these two narratives immediately become apparent, though. Seniors co-ops tackle isolation; single mother co-ops create space free from the threat of domestic abuse or landlord assault; Black co-ops create space for "solidarity and cultural/racial loyalty."[85] There is a lot of overlap between these two parallel narratives, and I argue this overlap occurs around the desire for self-determination.

A third foundational narrative is the interventionist humanitarianism by the economic elite. The conviction that through the bettering of the wage-earner's environment, there would be "no reason for animosity between man and man"[86] was central in shaping industrialist Robert Owen's vision for a planned town for his workers, which, as discussed earlier, later formed the basis of the co-op movement as it exists today.

Contemporary Radical Co-ops

There are some indications that the modern co-op housing movement does have some beacons of hope in the larger fight for citizen control and decommodified housing. Turning the focus back to the Communauté Milton-Parc, the most remarkable thing about its 15 housing co-ops is they have stayed true to the ideals of co-operative housing. Each and every member has to participate, all members serve on a committee, meeting minutes are distributed to everybody, all management is done from within the membership, there are no hired staff (other than paying an external auditor or contractors for renovations), and members are required to attend general assemblies. The strict responsibilities placed on members have paid off. Rents have stayed very low, evictions are extremely rare, and neighbourliness remains high. There are no landlords or property managers in the Milton-Parc co-ops and housing is more secure as a result.

Despite being created from the same government subsidy programs, the Milton-Parc co-ops stand in stark contrast to many housing co-ops in Ontario and elsewhere in Anglo-Canada, where participation is discouraged, committees are nonexistent, evictions are common, and transparency lacks.

This stark contrast can be attributed to two main factors. First, the Milton-Parc co-ops were specifically created to be small and manageable—the largest is 32 units. Of the ten goals and objectives listed in the community's 1980 Action Plan for Milton-Parc, number seven is, "Small groups will be formed to own and administer the properties." Second, the co-ops were formed on the basis of affinity—neighbours who knew and liked each other formed co-ops together. These two crucial factors were not adhered to in the development of the mainstream housing co-op movement across Canada.

The Fédération des coopératives d'habitation intermunicipale du Montréal métropolitain (FECHIMM), the regional Montreal housing co-op federation, severed its ties in 2014 with the provincial federation, the Confédération québécoise des coopératives d'habitation (CQCH). The FECHIMM members voted to withdraw their membership over the CQCH's approval of limited-equity co-ops, essentially opening the door to private, individual ownership, and what the FECHIMM called "a democratic deficit" (*déficit démocratique*). Also at play was the governance and voting structure, as the FECHIMM member co-ops represented almost half of the CQCH, but only 30% of the board.[87]

In the UK, there is a group of notably small, *à la* Milton-Parc, social justice oriented housing co-ops called Radical Roots. It is a "network of radical co-ops whose members are committed to working for positive social change. The network is made up mainly of housing co-ops of various sizes (none with more than 17 members), a few workers' co-ops and a couple of social centres." Radical Roots is not merely a scrappy group of small co-ops; it is structured around a community development framework. "Radical Routes is able to make loans to member co-ops due to our ethical investment arm, Rootstock. Radical Routes made its first loan in 1991, and since then has lent out over £573 000 to member co-ops without any bad debts from loans. Rootstock enables people to invest in grassroots co-operative projects while building on the unique track record of Radical Routes."[88]

In the US, co-ops have been used in the struggle for Black economic self-determination for a century.[89] More recently, with the implementation of the

"Jackson-Kush Plan" in Jackson, Mississippi as a platform to transform the majority Black, working class city into a solidarity economy emerged the vision of a network of co-ops and a community land trust. This vision, detailed in the 2017 book *Jackson Rising,* is also one based in historical narratives of using the co-op model for self-determination and to gain economic independence. Co-ops are the tool, as the Plan is based around the struggle against capitalism.

Cooperation Jackson, as the group working to implement this program is called, has put a lot of their efforts into big political wins. A big step forward was the election of Chokwe Lumumba as mayor of Jackson in 2013. Lumumba accomplished a lot in his time in office but unfortunately died eight months into his term. His son, Chokwe Antar Lumumba, is now the mayor of Jackson. Cooperation Jackson's focus on electoral campaigns, however, has come at the price of short-term, on-the-ground advances. But there are always trade-offs and Cooperation Jackson remains a revolutionary and realizable project.

Although there are positive strains of radicalism that exist in the co-op housing movement around the world, they are often at odds with the mainstream co-op movement, which favours almost total integration and adhesion to the capitalist economic order. In order for co-ops to truly be revolutionary and tools of self-determination, they need to be highly political and grounded in anticapitalist logic. If radicals are to use the co-op model, they need to be aware of the risk of co-optation and apoliticism that is rampant in the mainstream co-op movement. The kernel in the co-operative movement is powerful; it just remains to be seen how well it can be used to build an alternative world.

REFERENCES:

Akuno, Kali, Ajamu Nangwaya, and Cooperation Jackson. 2017. *Jackson Rising: The Struggle for Economic Democracy and Black Self-Determination in Jackson, Mississippi.* Daraja Press.

Apland, Lars, and Chris Axworthy. 1988. 'Collective and Individual Rights in Canada: A Perspective on Democratically Controlled Organizations'. *Windsor Yearbook of Access to Justice* 8: 44–80.

Bakunin, Mikhail Aleksandrovich, and Arthur Lehning. 1973. *Michael Bakunin: Selected Writings.* Writings of the Left. London: Jonathan Cape.

Birchall, Johnston. 1997. *The International Co-operative Movement.* Manchester, UK ; New York: Manchester University Press.

Butt, John, ed. 1971. *Robert Owen: Aspects of His Life and Work.* New York: Humanities Press.

CMHC (Canada Mortgage and Housing Corporation). 2011. 'Canadian Housing Observer 2011'. CMHC.

CHFC (Co-operative Housing Federation of Canada). 'Facts and Figures'. 2018. Accessed 1 April 2018. https://chfcanada.coop/about-co-op-housing/facts-and-figures/.

Chouinard, Vera. 1990. 'The Uneven Development of Capitalist States: 2. The Struggle for Cooperative Housing'. *Environment and Planning A* 22 (11): 1441–54. https://doi.org/10.1068/a221441.

Cole, Leslie. 2008. *Under Construction: A History of Co-operative Housing in Canada*. Ottawa: Borealis Press.

Corina, John Grenville. 1994. 'William King (1786-1865): Physician and Father of the Co-operative Movement'. *Journal of Medical Biography* 2: 168–76.

Coté, Mark, Richard Day, and Greig de Peuter. 2007. 'Utopian Pedagogy: Creating Radical Alternatives in the Neoliberal Age'. *Review of Education, Pedagogy, and Cultural Studies* 29 (4): 317–36. https://doi.org/10.1080/10714410701291129.

Craig, John G. 1993. *The Nature of Co-operation*. Montréal ; New York: Black Rose Books.

Day, Richard J. F. 2000. *Multiculturalism and the History of Canadian Diversity*. Toronto ; Buffalo: University of Toronto Press.

Day, Richard J. F. 2005. *Gramsci Is Dead: Anarchist Currents in the Newest Social Movements*. London ; Ann Arbor, MI : Toronto: Pluto Press; Between the Lines.

Dussel, Enrique. 2002. 'World-System and "Trans"-Modernity'. *Nepantla: Views from South* 3 (2): 221–44.

Errasti, Anjel. 2015. 'Mondragon's Chinese Subsidiaries: Coopitalist Multinationals in Practice'. *Economic and Industrial Democracy* 36 (3): 479–99. https://doi.org/10.1177/0143831X13511503.

Fairbairn, Brett. 1994. *The Meaning of Rochdale: The Rochdale Pioneers and the Co-operative Principles*. Occasional Paper Series, 94.02. Saskatoon, Sask., Canada: Centre for the Study of Co-operatives, University of Saskatchewan.

Fourier, Charles. 1971. *Design for Utopia: Selected Writings of Charles Fourier*. Vol. 10. Studies in the Libertarian and Utopian Tradition. New York: Schocken Books.

Fourier, Charles, Ian Patterson, and Gareth Stedman Jones. 1996. *The Theory of the Four Movements*. Cambridge Texts in the History of Political Thought. Cambridge: New York: Cambridge University Press.

Foucault, Michel, Michel Senellart, and Graham Burchell. 2009. *Security, Territory, Population: Lectures at the Collège de France, 1977-1978*. 1. Picador ed. New York: Picador.

Gordon Nembhard, Jessica. 2014. *Collective Courage: A History of African American Cooperative Economic Thought and Practice*. University Park, Pa: Pennsylvania State Univ. Press.

Graham, Robert. 2015. *We Do Not Fear Anarchy—We Invoke It*. Oakland, CA: AK Press.
Hands, John. 2016. *Housing Co-operatives*. London: Castleton.
Kaswan, Mark J. 2014. *Happiness, Democracy, and the Cooperative Movement: The Radical Utilitarianism of William Thompson*. Suny Series in New Political Science. Albany: State University of New York Press.
Kelly, Laura Rae. 2015. 'William Thompson and Anna Wheeler: Equality and Utilitarianism in the 19th Century'. PhD Thesis, Kingston, ON: Queen's University.
Lane, Fintan. 2010. *Politics, Society and the Middle Class in Modern Ireland*. Basingstoke, UK; New York: Palgrave Macmillan. http://www.palgraveconnect.com/doifinder/10.1057/9780230273917.
Lane, Fintan. Forthcoming. *William Thompson: The Life and Thought of a Radical, 1778-1833*. Bloomsbury.
Lichtheim, George. 1969. *The Origins of Socialism*. New York: Praeger.
Kasmir, Sharryn. 1996. *The Myth of Mondragón: Cooperatives, Politics, and Working-Class Life in a Basque Town*. SUNY Series in the Anthropology of Work. Albany: State University of New York Press.
Kasmir, Sharryn. 2016. 'The Mondragon Cooperatives and Global Capitalism: A Critical Analysis'. *New Labor Forum* 25 (1): 52–59. https://doi.org/10.1177/1095796015620424.
Kropotkin, Peter. 1902. *Mutual Aid: A Factor of Evolution*. 1902. http://dwardmac.pitzer.edu/Anarchist_Archives/kropotkin/mutaidcontents.html.
MacPherson, Ian. (n.d.). 'The history of the Canadian co-operative movement: A summary, a little historiography, and some issues'. Retrieved 1 April 2018. http://socialeconomyhub.ca/sites/socialeconomyhub.ca/files/Cdian%20Co-op%20History.doc
MacPherson, Ian. 1979. *Each for All*. Macmillan and Institute of Canadian Studies, Carleton University: Ottawa.
Marx, Karl. 1864. 'Inaugural Address of the International Working Men's Association'. 1864. https://www.marxists.org/archive/marx/works/1864/10/27.htm.
Marx, Karl. 1887. *Capital: Critique of Political Economy Volume I*. Accessed 1 April 2018. https://www.marxists.org/archive/marx/works/download/pdf/Capital-Volume-I.pdf
Mercer, T.W. 1922. 'The Life and Teaching of Dr. William King'. In *Dr. William King and the Co-operator, 1828-1830*. Manchester: The Co-operative Union Limited.
Mossing, Susan, and Shannon Salter. 2009. 'No Rights and No Review: How Housing Cooperatives Have Circumvented Procedural Fairness'. *The Advocate* 67 (4).

Naubauer, Ştefan. 2013. 'Predecessors and Perpetrators of Cooperative Systems in Europe'. *Lex et Scientia* XX (1): 40–50.

Ranis, Peter. 2016. *Cooperatives Confront Capitalism: Challenging the Neo-Liberal Economy*. London: Zed Books.

Ratner, Carl. 2013. *Cooperation, Community, and Co-ops in a Global Era*. International and Cultural Psychology. New York: Springer.

Ratner, Carl. 2015. *The Politics of Cooperation and Co-ops: Forms of Cooperation and Co-ops, and the Politics That Shape Them*. Capitalism, Counter-Capitalism, and Psychology. Hauppauge, New York: Nova Science Publisher's, Inc.

Schlemmer, Jeff. 2009. 'Deference" versus "Security of Tenure": Eviction of Residents of Subsidized Housing Co-Operatives at the Superior Court of Justice for Ontario, 1992-2009'. *Journal of Law and Social Policy* 22 (March): 43–67.

Simpson, Audra. 2014. *Mohawk Interruptus: Political Life across the Borders of Settler States*. Durham: Duke University Press.

Simpson, Leanne Betasamosake. 2017. *As We Have Always Done: Indigenous Freedom through Radical Resistance*. Indigenous Americas. Minneapolis: University of Minnesota Press.

Tawney, R.H. 1964. *The Radical Tradition*. New York: Pantheon.

Ward, Colin. 1990. *Talking Houses: Ten Lectures*. London: Freedom Press.

Ward, Colin. 1996. *Anarchy in Action*. London: Freedom Press.

Ward, Colin, Chris Wilbert, and Damian F. White. 2011. *Autonomy, Solidarity, Possibility: The Colin Ward Reader*. Oakland, CA: AK Press.

NOTES

1. Errasti 2015
1. Ward 1974, p. 49. Ward was quoting Lewis Waddilove, a well-known British proponent of housing co-ops.
2. Helman 1987, p. 108
3. Interview with Lucia Kowaluk, November 17, 2017
4. CHFC 2018
5. Data for these tables came from email correspondence with CHFC.
6. Social housing is defined by CMHC as "housing subsidized by governments (often developed in collaboration with the private and public not-for-profit sector) that is made available to those who would otherwise be unable to afford to live in suitable and adequate housing in the private market" (CMHC 2011, p. 127).
7. CMHC 2011, p. 128
8. Craig 1993, p. 11
9. Marx 1887, p. 230
10. Kropotkin 1902
11. Craig 1993, p. 19
12. MacPherson 1979, p. 3
13. Coté, Day & de Peuter 2007, p. 329

14 Simpson 2014, p. 44
15 Simpson 2017, p. 19
16 (Ibid.)
17 The Plain Language series of guide books was published by the Co-op Housing Bookstore, "a joint project of the Co-operative Housing Federation of Toronto and the Co-operative Housing Federation of   Canada."
18 MacPherson n.d., p. 3
19 CMHC 2003, p. 3
20 CMHC 1992, p. 2
21 Ibid.
22 Cole 2008
23 Ibid., ix
24 Ibid., p. 49
25 Ibid., p. 50
26 Genealogy here is used in the Foucault sense, "which reconstructs a whole network of alliances, communications, and points of support" (Foucault 2009, 117) and as a "move away from history as such…that offers new narratives with new kinds of social, political, and economic relations in mind" (Day 2005, 46).
27 In fact, as part of its liberal, free-market restructuring through perestroika and glasnost, the Soviet Union passed the "Law on Cooperatives" in 1988.
28 Craig 1993, p. 14
29 Ibid., p. 22
30 Kropotkin 1902
31 Butt 1071, p. 9
32 Thompson 1963, p. 784
33 Ibid., p. 782
34 Birchall 1997, p. 4; Fairbairn 1994, p. 6
35 Thompson 1963, p. 782
36 bid., p. 780
37 Butt 1971, p. 24
38 Tawney 1964, p. 36
39 Ibid., p. 16
40 Butt 1971, p. 14
41 Thompson 1963, p. 781
42 Tawney 1964, p. 38-39
43 Thompson 1964, p. 782)
44 Hetherington, Henry. 14 Jan 1832. Poor Man's Guardian. As cited in Butt 1971, p. 11
45 Thompson 1964, p. 784
46 Ibid.
47 The same point was raised at the Canadian Association for Studies in Co-operation's 2017 conference. Discussion around a "new co-operativism" was handily dismissed by a panelist, who argued the "new" prefix ignores huge social advancements made by individuals and groups through co-operatives.
48 Ibid.
49 MacPherson 1979, p. 3
50 Lichtheim 1969, p. 34
51 Fourier 1971, p. 66

52 Lichtheim 1969, p. 34
53 Naubauer 2013, p. 41
54 Day 2005, p. 105
55 Lichtheim 1969, p. 34
56 Day 2005, p. 106
57 Lichtheim 1969, p. 36
58 2013, p. 60
59 Kasmir 1996, p. 20–21
60 Fairbairn 1994, p. 6
61 Mercer 1922, p. xi
62 Birchall 1997, p. 4
63 Hands 2016, p. 24
64 Corina 1994, p. 170
65 Ibid., p. 172
66 See Kaswan 2014; Kelly 2015; Lane forthcoming; and Ranis 2016
67 Lane 2010, p. 21
68 Kelly 2015, p. 21
69 Ranis 2015, p. 9-11
70 Graham 2015, p. 95
71 Ranis 2016, p. 8
72 Marx 1864
73 Graham 2015, p. 64
74 Marx 1864
75 Graham 2015, p. 64
76 Bakunin 1973, p. 69-70
77 Ward 2011, p. 177
78 Ward 1996, p. 27
79 Ibid., p. 70-71
80 Coulthard 2007, p. 451
81 Tawney 1964, p. 39
82 Butt 1971, p. 22
83 Ward 1990, p. 121
84 Henderson 2011
85 Gordon Nembhard 2014, p. 217
86 Butt 1971, p. 23
87 See the FECHIMM's brochure titled, "Les faits sur la relation entre la FECHIMM et la CQCH"
88 http://www.radicalroutes.org.uk/
89 See Jessica Gordon Nembhard's excellent book *Collective Courage: A History of African American Cooperative Economic Thought and Practice*

Letter from Lucia Kowaluk to Phyllis Lambert and Heritage Montreal

April 18, 1979

Ms. Phyllis Lambert
Heritage Montreal
418 Bonsecours Street
Montreal

Dear Phyllis,

Enclosed is a statement of principles that has been discussed by the members of the prospective housing co-operative: Milton Parc. It offers guiding principles and suggestions that we hope will govern the management of the Paxmil properties at such time as your organization becomes the owner and/or manager of them.

About thirty people have approved of this statement, and it has been discussed over a period of four weeks.

We would like very much to meet with you to discuss it. We look forward to hearing your reactions and ideas, and to begin any implementation of the ideas, especially the suggestion of establishing a Board of Management which is stated on the last page of the document.

I guess I don't need to add that we are all very excited by the possibilities that this huge project offers, and we are eager to begin.

With best regards,

Lucia Kowaluk, for the Co-operative d'Habitation Milton Parc

P.S. We meet every Tuesday at 7:30 pm at 3749 Jeanne Mance. Could you come to our next meeting on April 26?

April 12, 1979
TO HERITAGE MONTREAL
Those of us Paxmil tenants who are interested in forming housing co-operatives with our homes feel the need to endorse a statement of principles which will both describe our vision of this neighbourhood, and will govern our negotiations with Heritage Montreal for the purchase and renovation of our homes, and for the continuing stability of our neighbourhood.

Starting at the macro-level with an understanding of the development of the urban fabric of Montreal, we feel that the land and streets of the Milton-Parc area (Paxmil houses) can play an essential role in maintaining a healthy residential quality to the Centre City. This area is northeast of the downtown. Beyond it for several miles to the north and the east are low-rise, low-cost residential neighbourhoods. Because the spread of private land and building development in any urban core is characterized by land speculation resulting in inflation, by greatly increased use-density, and by the destruction of traditional neighbourhoods, we feel it is important to check this spread. Without arguing the merits of this process for society as a whole, it does seem clear to us that to continue this process at this time in Montreal's development, and in this geographical direction, is destructive to the urban as a whole, and for all citizens of Montreal.

We elaborate these seemingly far-fetched points at this time because we feel that to stabilize our neighbourhood, to stop its deterioration, to freeze (relatively) its land values, to enhance its quality as a good residential area, and to retain its present mixed character regarding age, class, income and lifestyle is of benefit to Montreal as a whole, as well as to us, the present residents.

And to develop this argument along the micro-level, we feel that the establishment of housing co-operatives is the best way to achieve the objectives just stated above. Housing co-operatives stabilize land values, inhibiting land speculation, because they cannot be sold; rather they revert to the public domain if all their members leave. Because housing co-ops operate at no profit, and in addition receive generous subsidies at several levels of government, they give the opportunity to people of mixed income to live in the same neighbourhood, ensuring that all those who want to remain regardless of their income, may do so. Housing co-operatives offer the security and control of private ownership for those who do not have the money or interest in private ownership.

Having used this preamble to state our basic principles, we will go on to discuss specific points.

1. We believe that every effort should be made to establish housing co-operatives with the Paxmil housing. This means that aside from those people who have

already organized themselves to become members of co-ops, or to become private owners, those who have remained unresponsive to date, should be encouraged as much as possible to form co-ops.
- a. We ask that as part of the job of being managers, Heritage Montreal pay the salary of one or two organizers;
- b. We ask that Heritage Montreal do not sell any multiple-dwelling buildings to any profit-making individual or group. First a real effort must be made to help the present tenants to form a co-operative. If present tenants are not interested, then efforts will be made to find non-profit owners such as church groups who will run group homes or the like. We cannot approve the use of public monies to gain advantages on property which then will be passed on to individuals who will use it for private profit. We insist that Heritage Montreal remain the owner and manager of such property until another non-profit arrangement can be made.
- c. We ask that no autonomous lodging—that is any lodging with its own civic street number—be sold to a person who does not plan to live in that lodging.
- d. We ask that no person not presently living in a Paxmil dwelling be eligible to buy any Paxmil property until it is reasonably certain that no present Paxmil tenant is interested in the property either as an individual or as a member of a co-operative. Under no conditions should any tenant be asked to leave.
- e. We ask that where there is a conflict regarding the future of a duplex or a triplex, and every effort at an amiable solution has failed, that Heritage Montreal favour selling the building to a co-op.
- f. We ask that existing co-operatives have the right of first refusal on the future sale of any property bought by a present resident at the price the owner paid plus his expenses.

2. We urge the clarification of the financial arrangements and the stipulations of CMHC as soon as possible.
   - a. We are not clear as to the interest rates that will be charged to the co-ops and to private owners.
   - b. We assume that the initial grant from CMHC covers purchase price and renovation. We feel that the plan for renovating the houses should strike a balance between the desirability of individual control over renovation, and the need to immediately upgrade the face of the neighbourhood as well as to make certain essential repairs. We ask therefore, that Heritage Montreal undertake immediately the renovation of the OUTSIDES of the

houses which would include: roofs, windows, wall insulation, repairs and repainting of all exterior woodwork and doors, repairs and fire-proofing or demolition of all exterior stairs and sheds, repairs of structural problems.

These repairs would assure: 1) the most economical prices; 2) that the whole area which is very dirty and deteriorated immediately look better; 3) that the cost of certain very costly repairs be equalized, and 4) that no one owner be allowed to spoil the general look of the neighbourhood by not repairing his house.

The interior renovations can be done more slowly and according to individual standards and taste within CMHC regulations.

3. Since Heritage Montreal will own and manage the properties for a certain period of time (up to 5 years of more), we would like to suggest certain guidelines.
   a. We should try to get within the community the resources and evaluations. They should be formed, according to the needs and dimensions of the community.
   b. The present maintenance crew working for Paxmil has shown itself to be very knowledgeable about the properties and neighbourhood. We ask, therefore, that they be retained to continue their work.
   c. We have been working closely with the CDLC who are very knowledgeable on questions of co-ops, renovations and government programs. We ask that they be formally hired as consultants to help us with the management of these properties.
   d. We ask that a Board of Directors be established to direct the management of the properties. This Board would fairly represent all the preponderant interests involved: tenants at large, co-op members, resident owners, Heritage Montreal, maintenance and management crew, and any others as many seem to fairly deserve representation. This Board would be privy to all pertinent information and would make decisions affecting its members. The details of this Board would have to be worked out. This Board would establish a system of renting to people not already Paxmil tenants in such a way as to favour people committed to the formation of co-ops.

Social Production of Habitat: The Emergence of a Paradigm Shift in the Making of Cities

Iman Salama

ACCORDING TO MANY analysts and experts, the world is facing an unprecedented shortage of affordable housing. Cities from all over the world, in developing and advanced economies alike, are struggling to meet that need. Since the early 1980s, many governments have withdrawn from any territorial planning, leaving the market to freely operate the private appropriation of urban spaces, with little restrictions to real-estate speculation. Public policies tend to accentuate this situation by increasingly defining housing as merchandise and human habitat as a business, leaving millions of people with little or no options. As a result, inequalities are increasing both in the so-called *developed* and *developing* countries.

While governments are struggling to find innovative ways to address the housing shortage, thousands of homes are being built daily, and communities across the world are coming up with creative and collective solutions to respond to their needs. Between 50 and 75% of human settlements in developing countries are the result of people's own initiatives and efforts with very little support from governments and experts. The so-called slums are self-built neighborhoods outside of government programs that develop incrementally over time from small villages to densely populated areas and are built by a variety of experienced local actors. A lot of the illegitimate views of these dynamics exist because it is taught that residents don't own the land they occupy. In developed countries, speculation has also left many families outside of the affordable housing market. A diversity of community-led housing initiatives is emerging across Europe and North America where land speculation and social disparities are increasingly pushing communities into exploring new democratic alternatives for the provision of housing, urban infrastructure, social services and collective land ownership.

What is less known is that, at a global level, these popular forms of production are the norm rather than the exception. Entire cities have been developed outside of official plans, through collective agency and built by various actors. In fact, the binaries between the formal and the informal cannot be understood as absolute. These are working terminologies of a much more complex urban reality and economic, social and political dynamics. Many current urban regulations ignore or make illegal people's individual and collective efforts to obtain a decent place to live and in most cases, they come up against many barriers. What these collective and individual initiatives, formal or informal, are lacking is a better understanding of their processes and support through a framework providing better planning on many levels. In fact, when considering planning practices and policies, there is very little said about the distinct responsibility of various social actors, experts, and local governments or about the possibilities to transform the process of housing production and urban planning.

However, today the theoretical construct of contemporary cities seems to be evolving. In recent years, the planning process has assumed a more scientific status and the theory and practice of planning is more relevant to current challenges of society. Social participation in sustainable development, poverty reduction, social justice, and democracy have caused the planning field to open up to ordinary people as part of the solution in which participatory strategies are becoming central to the process. In fact, the planner's current *nostrum* for bringing reform to the field is citizen participation, and the implementation of a wide range of participatory approaches has been added to the growing volume of literature about planning. Planning practice is also more and more in line with Jane Jacobs' long-standing argument that economic development comes from enabling local communities to solve their own problems and create their own opportunities. Yet can we say that a methodology centred around participation in planning is itself enough, or are changes to social decision-making processes and resource distribution also required?

Defining Social Production of Habitat as a People-Centered Planning Process

Learning to look at cities through their social networks of production is not new. John F.C. Turner, an architect who worked in Lima in the 1960s, spent his professional life studying the way people provided for their own housing needs using their know-how and locally available resources. He wanted to explore how planners and architects could support those processes, rather than impose their own solutions. His ideas were in fact very influential and since the 1970s his concept of self-help in housing has become a strong theoretical foundation and a practical and functional basis for public policies and interventions. People were encouraged to build their own dwellings on land provided by the State and equipped with basic infrastructure. However, prices in the real estate sector kept rising and continue to boom to this day, and public land became too valuable to simply let people occupy and build on it. Most importantly, practices inspired by the concept of self-help withdrew the notion of "user control" over the construction process, which led to their failure in achieving the concept's original objective as viewed by Turner, allowing for integrated community participation and the creation of autonomy in housing environments.

The social production of habitat (SPH) is an international concept that first appeared in the 1960s in Latin America, also based on observations of emergent community groups driving innovative and self-managed experiences in responding to their basic housing needs. Habitat International Coalition (HIC), an independent non-profit alliance, has been working on and promoting this concept for more than 30 years. The coalition includes social movements, community-based organizations, support groups and academics, all of which are dedicated in the advocacy for a sustainable habitat for all. For Enrique Ortiz, HIC president from 2003 to 2007, "social production of habitat encompasses both the process and product arising from people's collective initiative at building their own habitat: dwellings, villages, neighbourhoods, and even large parts of the cities." In contrast to an understanding of participation, where people are sporadically involved at certain points of the planning process and not in others, SPH is a concept that places people at the center of the planning process, one that allows for user-control over the entire project with decision-making power over the design, planning, financing, and management of the project.

SPH defines housing as a process rather than a product. As opposed to merchandise, housing has a social and cultural value and is an act of inhabiting rather than an object of exchange. Its values lie in the interaction between the actors, their activities and the house and imply various levels of social participation in the housing production phases that include the planning, construction, distribution, and use. This experience of people collectively determining the conditions of their own habitat also implies their capacity to articulate essential resources such as land, local construction materials, financial and human capital, expertise and building tools. In fact, in SPH experiences, there is a greater dependence on people's capacity to negotiate land prices and the process of acquiring and transferring property rights, accessing tools and materials, financial resources, and architectural expertise. These resources are a function of law and its administration, which raises questions about the necessary framework for enabling, supporting and strengthening popular processes in the production of cities and urges urban practitioners to rethink the roles of architects and planners, governments and communities alike.

Building an International Support Network for Social Production of Habitat

Today, many community initiatives around the world are leading experimentation in new forms of participatory governance, housing provision, land ownership and the collaborative economy. Those experiences are beginning to acquire much wider visibility and acknowledgment in particular under the concept of SPH, which is growing internationally. urbaMonde, a Swiss NGO dedicated to promoting sustainable cities by and for the inhabitants of Geneva, has started working on this concept with HIC. In 2014, they co-organized a first International Forum on Social Production of Habitat gathering projects from all over the world. The aim of such an event was to create a space for discussion over the thematic convergence of various community-led projects from different countries all providing innovative and sustainable solutions to the housing crisis and land insecurity, as well as social, economic and spatial inequalities in cities.

This meeting point was a strategic encounter between different regional networks sharing the same vision and all coming together under the umbrella of the social production of habitat. Among the participants, four regional networks attended the event: Slum Dweller International (SDI), a global social movement of the urban poor in 33 countries across Africa, Asia and Latin America; Asian Coalition for Housing Rights (ACHR), a regional network of grassroots community organizations, NGOs and professionals involved in urban poor development processes; Co-operative Housing International (CHI), an alliance promoting co-operative housing as a solution to shelter in all countries; and National Community Land Trust Network (NCLTN), which inspires action and reform policies that help create equitable housing opportunities for all. They were among the first to partner with urbaMonde and HIC in the creation of an international platform for social production of habitat to join forces and build exchange programs.

The SPH platform seeks to develop peer-to peer exchange between projects, provide them with technical and financial support, increase documentation on community-led housing experiences, and capitalize on existing projects through various media to advocate for public policy on different scales. Its objective is to develop common tools to support emergent projects around the world and strengthen the capacities of communities by creating a global network of solidarity. Indeed, the fact that SPH is people-centered does not mean that communities can do everything on their own. Partners in SPH can be informal groups or local organizations, or other actors external to the community, such as NGOs, donors, co-operatives, private sector enterprises, professionals, academics, government institutions or any combination of these. They play a crucial role in providing communities with adequate resources to plan and manage their projects.

The platform documents innovative models for each phase of a community-led housing project. According to the observations, those include six main steps: the way a community organizes itself; strategies to negotiate and access land;

obtaining technical and architectural expertise for planning; pooling financial resources; building the project; and managing the whole process. Those steps are indivisible and are all part of the overall planning process that community-led projects are engaged in. Depending on local needs and the nature and scale of a project as well as its social, cultural, economic and political context, innovative solutions may focus on one of those aspects more than others. For instance, when in a situation of poverty, saving groups are models that allow communities to raise common financial resources that are collectively managed to undergo their projects. It also strengthens social cohesion between people, which is at the heart of a community planning process and its capacity to mobilize and take action under a shared vision. In other contexts where projects exceed the financial capacity of most inhabitants, communities need to attract external public and private funding at favorable conditions that allows for sustainable solutions while maintaining control over the process. This is why other initiatives will also focus on democratic governance and anti-speculation.

In fact, whatever their focus is, access to and the management of land will remain a major issue for community-led housing projects. SPH projects present various strategies for negotiating land that shows how challenging it is for communities to be in concurrence with public or private real estate interests. Examples of Community Land Trust models aim to pull land off the property market, such as in the Champlain Housing Trust in the US where inhabitants own the house they live in, on land rented from the Trust. In Latin America, the FUCVAM, a federation of mutual aid housing co-operatives, has negotiated with the State to create a mechanism for the public acquisition of land by co-operatives at accessible prices. In Canada, the Communauté Milton-Parc (CMP), the non-profit organization behind a unique land ownership structure, owns the common land in a downtown Montreal neighbourhood, while its member housing co-operatives and non-profit housing associations own their respective buildings and the land directly underneath. A co-ownership declaration was drafted by the CMP to guarantee the non-speculative use of those spaces by abolishing private ownership so that inhabitants become co-responsible for the permanent protection of land as a common good.

While these are only a few examples of projects that are documented through the SPH platform, many others are out there, in many countries, presenting interesting solutions or seeking to mobilize their communities to initiate a project. This is why a last-but-not-least phase of the SPH process is the sharing of experience. Because the know-how acquired in one part of the world can inspire others on a local, national and international scale, the platform also aims at connecting those initiatives with each other. Although the documentation in itself capitalizes on this knowledge, in order to facilitate those exchanges, the platform has, in partnership with Building and Social Housing Foundation (BSHF), developed an SPH award in relation to the World Habitat award. The award offers financial support to foster human interactions and peer-to-peer exchange between community-led projects and their main players with field visits and training programs that allow for the direct dissemination of alternative building techniques and organizational, managerial and financial housing models between community groups.

Besides the exchange programs, building regional networks of mutual aid and knowledge exchange contributes to the expansion and strengthening of the SPH movement, giving it greater national and international visibility as part of a major advocacy for public support mechanisms.

Towards Local and Global Advocacy for Support Policies and the Right to Land

SPH experiences are different in form, scale and strategies and their specific needs depend on their contexts, making it hard to draw common solutions. However, whatever the context is, SPH advocates for an effective transformation of local and national policies towards understanding and supporting people's processes for access and provision of land and housing. Common features and principles can be drawn in the sense that the community's participation in the production of their living environments calls for a redistribution of social goods and opportunities and will appear as a new, essential approach to housing accessibility within the framework of public policies.

It is therefore essential to understand the forces that strengthen or weaken people's processes. Self-management and finance, participative responsibility, exercising direct-democracy and local governance contribute to strengthening community practice. Governments, social organizations and technical experts should develop innovative and efficient use of the financial and political resources to formulate public policies, toolkits, support mechanisms, programs and plans based on people's practices and their specific needs.

There are also many obstacles that limit the work of communities and their capacity to carry out a project. In some cases poor information on rights, low education levels, weak organizational and management capacities, or even the low social and economic conditions which families are in can create a lot of insecurities. It is therefore crucial to understand that legal, financial and administrative tools relevant to self-managed processes, greater attention to low-income sectors, and effective land tenure security have to be part of the promotion of SPH processes. At the very least, State obligations need to abstain from actions that would harm the SPH, such as forced evictions. To protect themselves from the speculative market and forced evictions, what many advocates of SPH are promoting are policies and housing models in which the individual property is not the only possibility. The collective dimension of housing, and the diversity of forms of land ownership, are highlighted as alternative models that protect them against private property and its negative effects. In fact, many urban struggles against eviction are putting forward access to affordable housing as a basic human right.

It is not a surprise that promoting the central role of civil society and the variety of tools they develop to negotiate land is seen as directly linked to the housing crisis. Raquel Rolnick, the previous United Nations special rapporteur on adequate housing, addresses the access to land as a central element of the right to adequate housing. In her report called *Guiding Principles on Security of Tenure for the urban poor*, presented to the Human Rights Council in December 2013, she states that "the concept of legitimate tenure rights extends beyond mainstream notions of private ownership and includes multiple tenure forms deriving from a variety of tenure systems." In a context of disinvestment of public housing stock and communities being subject to rapid gentrification, she explicitly speaks about the importance of diversifying tools to negotiate land as a pressing human rights issue.

Access to land is also fundamental to the right to the city (RTC), a concept which was first proposed by Henri Lefebvre in his book *Le Droit à la ville* in 1968. Following in his footsteps, today the global platform for the right to the city is a movement that emerged from the coming together of many organizations around the world which are using the concept as a call to action to reclaim the city as a co-created space. Its objective is to push national and local governments and international and regional organizations towards a "new paradigm for a more inclusive and democratic urban development."

The concept had particular influence in Latin America and Europe where social movements have promoted local instruments for advancing practical understanding in terms of policy-making on local and national levels. Some cities already have charters that include this concept. The Mexico City Charter for the Right to the City was negotiated with the Federal District in 2007 by popular movements. It is structured around guiding principles which implicate the improvement of individual and collective living conditions through the management, production and responsible development of the city such as "the full exercise of human rights in the city; the social function of the city, of land, and of property; democratic management of the city; democratic production of the city and in the city; sustainable and responsible management of natural, heritage, and energy resources of the city and its surroundings; and democratic and equitable enjoyment of the city."

Platforms such as the RTC platform and the SPH platform are capitalizing on and using those experiences as advocacy tools for enabling public-policies, helping them gain international recognition in many urban forums such as

Habitat III, United Cities and Local Governments (UCLG), World Urban Forum (WUF) and World Social Forum (WSF). Today, the RTC and the SPH are advanced concepts which are lobbied for adoption as central focus points of the United Nations Sustainable Development Goals and the New Urban Agenda, calling for practical enabling policies that build on collective agency and improve access to resources.

In this respect, the claims of SPH are a component of the RTC and close to the content of the human right to adequate housing, which already embodies the claim for a number of rights at once. This is why the discourse surrounding SPH and access to land encompasses the only question of housing and land. The true issue is one that concerns the urban space, its distribution, the economy and the decentralization of political power over decision-making. It calls for structural changes in governance and the need to support social movements and all the concerned parties including State officials and professionals to collectively improve living conditions in our cities.

From Urban Villages to Cities from the Bottom-Up

The challenge of social production of habitat lies in scale. Today, beyond public consultation as a minimal form of participation, which is usually a static and frustrating experience for people and professionals alike, meaningful community participation as active partners in shaping cities is still making its way in public policies. In a context of global mass urbanization and transformation in planning culture, the values of those ideas are of great significance and offer new insights on the relevance of social production of habitat as a new paradigm in urban planning, one in which the process of producing housing and neighbourhoods requires a shift from top-down planning to bottom-up processes to become a transformative movement towards sustainable, just and resilient cities.

REFERENCES

Turner, John F. C. 1976. *Housing by People: Towards Autonomy in Building Environments*. Ideas in Progress. London: Marion Boyars.
urbaMonde. 2014. *Production Sociale de l'Habitat*.
Habitat International Coalition. 2005. *Social Production of Habitat: Reflections on rights, policies, and perspectives for regional and global advocacy*.
Habitat International Coalition. 2010. *Mexico Right to the City Charter*.
Social production of habitat platform: www.psh.urbamonde.org
Right to the city platform: www.righttothecityplatform.org

1983 CMHC Press Release on the Inauguration of Milton-Parc

Communiqué News Release
Source: Canada Mortgage and Housing Corporation
Quebec Regional Office
For Immediate Release

MILTON PARK:
Canada's Most Important Cooperative Renovation Project

Montreal, September 23rd, 1983—Andre Ouellet, minister of labor in the Canadian government, in company of Serge Joyal, secretary of state, David Berger, M.P. for Laurier and Jacques Guilbault, M.P. for St-Jacques, proceeded today at the inauguration of Milton Parc.

Also present was Robert Montreuil, president of Canada Mortgage and Housing Corporation (CMHC) and several representatives of the other levels of government.

The Milton Park project is considered the most ambitious and important housing renovation plan ever to be done in Canada. These 135 buildings, totaling 600 housing units are the core of the project. They are situated between des Pins Avenue to the north, Milton to the south, Ste-Famille to the east and Hutchison to the west.

In 1979, at the request of Milton Park residents threatened with expulsion in the wake of ambitious urban renewal projects plan for their neighborhood, the federal government, acting through CMHC, acquired 135 buildings in Milton Park for 5,5 million $. This gave to some 2000 residents of the neighborhood time to get organized into housing cooperatives and non-profit associations, thus acquiring the necessary tools for taking control of their area before it was submitted to even greater speculation.

The citizens of Milton Park, who today have reclaimed their renovated housing at a price not higher than the scale they were paying before work began on the project, benefited in their fight from the help of a whole series of groups.

Among them, the sustained efforts of the Société du Patrimoine urbain de

Montréal (SPUM) and of the Société d'amélioration Milton Parc (S.A.M.P.) should be stressed. It should also be noted that CMHC handed over property rights to S.A.M.P., notwithstanding a balance on the sales price and other charges of nearly 7 million $. S.A.M.P. is presently managing the project in trust, awaiting the transfer of ownership by which coop members and non-profit associations will become co-owners of their homes.

Total monies invested in this 597-unit housing project, which also includes twenty or more neighborhood shops, have been estimated at 30 660 731$.

The realization of a cooperative project of this size could not have been possible without financial assistance from CMHC. The latter has in fact guaranteed mortgage loans evaluated at 24 310 000$ at 100% of their value, to allow the purchase and renovation of these homes. The Corporation also paid out grants totaling 3 042 614$ to help cooperatives get started, to provide the necessary technical help and to assist housing renovation. Moreover, it also assigned another grant of 306 670$ as part of its program to assist demonstration projects.

Finally, following section 56.1 of the N.H.A.[1], CMHC promises to come up with another grant aimed at keeping rents at a reasonable cost. Following the provisions of the present agreement, this assistance will mean annual payments of 3 900 000$, or a total commitment for the Canadian government of 138 810 000$ over the next 35 years. Thus, unit rental costs varying from 323$ to 1 235$, according to today's market, will be lowered to a range of from 123$ to 367$ per unit, depending on the size of the dwelling and the income of its occupants.

MILTON PARK: Historical Background

Built at the turn of the century for the well-to-do, The Milton Park neighborhood had maintained its residential character into the 1950s and encompassed a variety of dwellings, most of them inhabited by families. Over the years, the aging of these houses had gradually forced out the well-to-do community, who were replaced by other families, single people and senior citizens, with low or moderate incomes. The almost century-old neighborhood offered them a complete range of services at hand-hospitals, churches, schools, shops, recreational parks—all this a few minutes from downtown.

Towards the end of the 1950s, Milton Park's strategic location became a perfect target for promoters wanting to maximize the profitability of rare downtown properties. Thus, during the mid-1960s, part of the neighborhood was bought up by Concordia Estates Ltd., which intended to build an ambitious urban renewal project.

At the beginning of the 1970s, the demolition of 250 housing units inaugurated work on the Concordia project. Neighborhood residents were not slow to react to this onslaught and created the Comité des citoyens de Milton Parc (or Milton Park Citizens' Committee) to make themselves heard and attempt to preserve their homes and their neighborhood.

In 1973, construction began on Concordia's Cité project and its promoters handed over the houses which had so far escaped demolition to PAXMILL.

In March, 1978, a group of citizens seeking to found a housing cooperative expressed their desire to become buyers of PAXMILL's properties.

In January 1979, getting wind of the situation, Héritage Montréal urged CMHC to buy the project. On the 25th of April, 1979, CMHC announced to the press its intention to comply with the Milton Park residents' wishes. Thus, in May, 1979, CMHC signed a letter of intent with the S.P.U.M. to become owner of the project for a sum of 5,5 million $

Following the Canadian government's housing policy, CMHC accepted, in October 1979, the Action Plan devised by S.P.U.M., in collaboration with Milton Park residents, enabling them to reoccupy their dwellings, after renovation, without having to pay proportionally more rent than before.

Today, Milton Park is made up of 135 buildings totally 597 homes plus a score of neighborhood shops. A population of nearly 2 000 people grouped into some 20 associations have re-taken possession of their housing. Milton Park will have cost 30 660 731$ and, according to prevailing market prices, rents should vary from 323$ to 1 235$ per unit per month. Thanks to the concerted efforts and the financial assistance of CMHC, Canada's housing agency, the rental scale paid by Milton Park residents is presently between 123$ and 367$ per unit, depending on the size of the unit and the income of its occupants.

Administrative and Technical Organization

Milton Park properties are presently administered in trust by the S.P.U.M. until such time as coop members and non-profit groups become the co-owners and managers of the project.

Created by Héritage Montréal, S.P.U.M. then created the S.A.M.P. and the Groupe de resources techniques Milton Parc ("Technical Resources Group of Milton Park", or G.R.T). These three non-profit organizations played a technical, administrative and organizational support role among Milton Park citizens for the duration of the project.

The two first groups bring together, on a voluntary basis, advisory experts in town planning, architecture, financing, property management, law and cooperatives. As well, Milton Park G.R.T. is made up of animation, architectural, administration, and training services for the duration of the project. It is worth remembering that this group is financed through CMHC's community resources organization program. To these main groups are occasionally added numerous consultants: appraisers, chartered accountants, insurance experts, lawyers, notaries and town planners.

Moreover, a non-profit group, the Société de développement communautaire Milton Parc[2], manages the 20 or so shops in the neighborhood.

NOTES

1. Section 56.1 of the National Housing Act was the Non-profit And Cooperative Housing Program
2. The SDC remains part of the Communauté Milton-Parc and is responsible for managing the commercial properties.

An Interview with Dimitrios Roussopoulos

Editor's Note: This interview with Dimitri Roussopoulos, conducted by Francesca Ammon, Assistant Professor of City and Regional Planning at the University of Pennsylvania School of Design, took place on July 12, 2017 in Montreal. It was part of a research project Ammon undertook for the Canadian Centre for Architecture's Multidisciplinary Research Program: Architecture and/for Photography, entitled "Captioning Milton-Parc."

Francesca Ammon: When did you first become involved in the Milton-Parc area?
Dimitri Roussopoulos: It was 1962 or 1963 on Sainte-Famille. We rented a three-floor building—actually, it was a former residence, and it was owned by the then developers, Concordia Estates Ltd. We rented it from them and we opened up the Montreal Peace Centre. It was a hub of the protest culture of the 1960s.
FA: When you rented from Concordia, did you know that their plans were to demolish the neighbourhood?
DR: No, of course not.
FA: Did you receive communication from them since you were renting?
DR: Not at all.
FA: How did you learn about their plans?
DR: The Concordia Estates gang were a bunch of creatures who politically cohabitated the upper echelons of the Quebec Communist Party in the 1950s. In 1956, all three of them, the top dogs of Concordia, went through a traumatic experience when they learned that Stalin was not such a good guy after all. This traumatized a lot of Communist members, and these three characters decided to leave the Communist Party and cross the street. So they said, "Well, maybe capitalism is not that bad after all," and they apparently—or a few of them—went into the real estate business. A few years after, so the story goes, they started buying up property in this rundown part of the city and they came up with a strategic plan, otherwise known as a business plan or whatever you want to call it. They started buying every possible house they could in this six-block area with a view of developing it.

They were quite clever. They got money from this place and that place. The Ford Foundation gave them money because they sold it as an urban renewal project; the British Post Office gave them money from their union fund; and one of the biggest insurance companies in Winnipeg, Great West Life, gave them money. They just got money here and there to help buy this area. Even though they were "politically educated," being big honchos in the Communist Party, they were in fact politically very stupid because they had their big public announcement, their big press conference, in 1968.

1968, in a nutshell, was the major accumulation of what happened in the whole decade of the 1960s, and there were massive uprisings throughout the United States. There were several assassinations. There were uprisings in Mexico, in Tokyo, in Paris, and so on and so forth. There's a whole literature of that.

And of course, we here—the generation of the 1960s—were very much attuned to what was happening elsewhere and significant things were taking place here. When they announced their City of the 21st Century, it wasn't that difficult to turn the spark into a flame. The people at the University Settlement—who were mostly social workers at the McGill School of Social Work, and who under the influence of people like Lucia Kowaluk and other social workers, immediately realized what was happening and what was at stake—started the first series of organizational meetings.

The 1960s celebrated two major radical ideas. One was community organizing: you bring together people under the rubric of community organizing so that the underclass—what was referred to as the underclass, as opposed to the working class or the middle class or the upper class—the underclass learn how to work together in order to defend their rights and in order to protect their communities. People at the McGill School of Social Work—people like Saul Alinsky came to teach there, and Stokely Carmichael was a speaker there. There were all sorts of interesting speakers that people brought to McGill to speak and so on. These ideas percolated all over the place. Community organizing was one of the major streams of the new radicalism of the 1960s.

The other major stream was a belief that liberal democracy was wanting, that we were not at all happy with a democracy of consent, which was putting a piece of paper in a box every four years. We wanted a democracy of participation, where ordinary people had a word to say on what their lives were all about and what they wanted their communities and society to be all about. That second stream was characterized with the words "participatory democracy."

When the Milton-Parc Citizens' Committee was created, these two ideas fused together and we said, in effect, we are going to prevent this from happening. That's how the battle began.

FA: So the announcement took place and immediately the community organized?

DR: Well, I wouldn't say the community organized. I would say a very skilled and thoughtful minority around a social agency started the ball rolling. Lucia tells a story that the first person who found out about it was a woman by the name of Florence Bailin. Florence was a social worker at the University Settlement. The way it is described is that Florence almost ran into the University Settlement on Saint-Urbain Street and said, "They want to destroy the neighbourhood! They want to destroy the neighbourhood!"

The second floor of the University Settlement, which is where these other people were working, said, "What? What? Tell us about it." So immediately heads started to get together. They knew what had to be done initially. First of all there was a ready constituency around the University Settlement. It was a community centre with social services, and so people were coming in every day, and the gossip mill went into high gear. "They want to destroy our neighbourhood. They want to do this. They want to build luxurious apartment buildings. We have to stop this. How do we do it?"

FA: What were the first tactics for opposing this?
DA: Door-to-door work. Talking to people.

One of the skills that even the most moderate of social workers had is the ability to talk. They are congenital talkers. Whether it's a telephone or person-to-person, they love talking. All these people: Florence Bailin, Sue White, Ron Schulman, Bryan Knight, Peter Katadotis, and on and on—these people were out knocking on doors.

Starting a movement of ideas is like an election campaign. You have to talk to people directly. Once you get a sense of what is out there, then you call for public information meetings, which calls for a whole set of other means to get people to come out of their house and go to another place to sit in a chair and listen to updates on what is happening.

FA: At that point in time, the notion of co-ops and renovation didn't yet exist in people's minds?

DR: No, what we wanted to do was preventive action. We wanted to prevent that project from going forward. With time, we began thinking: what is part of our vision for down the road? One of the things we discussed was, well, these houses are not in the best of shape. They need to be renovated. With a freshness and innocence of youth, I remember drafting a letter. We sent a letter to every single architect in Montreal. We asked for their help.

Only one replied. But that one architect was worth his weight in gold. His name was Michael Fish. Not only did he reply, not only did he offer to come to look at the buildings, but he worked out that it would be more expensive to demolish and put up new buildings than to renovate them. By about five to eight dollars per square foot at the time.

When that information became available to the Milton-Parc Citizens' Committee, we said, "Well, even under capitalist terms, it makes sense that this neighbourhood has to be saved." Although we were not focused on greystones and architecture and that stuff—we just wanted to save people's homes.

FA: Were there some people focused on saving the buildings for heritage?

DR: No. This is 1968 and 1969. Heritage wasn't on the agenda. Heritage only became an issue with the birth of Save Montreal and the demolition of the Van Horne mansion.

These were people who loved the neighbourhood. They knew it was well-placed, they loved the shops, they loved the people—or most of the people. That was the main motive. Once we started understanding the whole economics of renovation, as opposed to demolition, the idea started germinating of building a movement. Not only a defensive movement, but a movement that had a vision behind it. The vision included the realization of various projects: we started a legal clinic, a credit union, and a daycare. We started projects and institutions that helped create a sense of who we are, what we wanted, and the society in which we wanted to live, and then began an awareness of what co-operation means and what a co-op could mean. Also, co-ops hardly existed in those times.

More than wanting to change the housing into co-operatives, we wanted to create a co-operative community. That's very important. A co-operative community, a co-operative society, that shared certain common values. It's very important to understand that.

When we fought to save the neighbourhood, we fought for something that was a very powerful, forward-looking vision of the transformation of society, and that made so much sense coming out of the 1960s.

And the thing rolled forward. When you look back at it now, it could be characterized as full of radical actions but they were so much part of the protest culture of 1960s.

You would have difficulties appreciating the fact that when you demonstrated in those days, that was considered controversial. In those days, demonstrating was a real commitment, and so a whole new culture was born in the area and it grew and as it got attention.

What is also very interesting, because it was the 1960s and into the 1970s, it also attracted the support of the Francophone left.

The Confederation of National Trade Unions' construction union gave us its solid support. They were prepared to think of building something new based upon a whole different approach to what should be built and where.

Amongst the Francophones, there was a growing solidarity with Milton-Parc.

FA: What about some of the older residents? Was there pushback from them, that this was never going to work, it was too radical?

DR: There were those kinds of people, to be sure, but there were others who were supportive. I'll tell you one of the psychological transformations that allowed that to happen. There was another remarkable architect who taught at McGill, who wound up being the Dean of Architecture at Laval University and who was very committed to the kind of housing we wanted. He was English and was part of the Labour Left. So he understood the ideas, the social ideas, and when he was at McGill he had a project which was called the Community Design Workshop. His name was Joe Baker, and he got his students to build a maquette of a Milton-Parc project that was converted into co-operatives, and the exhibit was put on display. I remember it as if it happened yesterday. People would be coming in and saying, "Oh look, there's my house. Is that the way it's going to look?"

It became something visual and very real. And we talked about it. We had drawings on the walls. But still a lot people just didn't believe it was going to happen. Just pie in the sky kind of thing.

The Concordia Estates Ltd. project had three phases to it. They managed to do phase one, and phases two and three were saved. They demolished a very significant row of houses between Jeanne-Mance and Parc Avenue on Prince Arthur, the northern side. Those buildings were emptied out and we occupied them. That occupation was quite significant because we took over these empty buildings, we put flowers in the windows, cleaned them up, and a certain number of older residents came to us with flowers and with food.

Joe Baker's efforts, our occupation of Prince Arthur and our constant door-knocking and keeping a human contact with people was extremely important in weaving together a sense of what could happen.

All of that came to a head not with the demolition, but with the fact that we couldn't do anything more to convince the political and economic establishment and the Concordia people to give in, and so we decided to occupy their offices on Parc Avenue. That actually is what crowned the name Milton-Parc, because it was on Milton and Parc, the occupation. We occupied it and we were 59 people.

FA: This is the arrest.

DR: There was a huge crowd outside, including members of this construction union. The head of them came, a very remarkable man by the name of Michel Bourdon, to show their support. People like Lucia were there with our son who was around three years old. The police had cordoned it off. The paddy wagons came, and the police officer said to Lucia, "You know, we're going to arrest people inside the circle. So since you have that little boy, maybe you'd like to go outside of the circle?" Which is what she did. But they didn't arrest people in the circle, in the end. They arrested people in the building and sitting on the staircase, the outside staircase.

It was very interesting. You went inside, you sat down on the floor. One of the people who was there was a very, very extraordinary woman by the name of Claire Culhane. She had a remarkable personal history. She was a Communist sympathizer, but she abandoned that and she became a professional nurse. She decided to go to Vietnam to do nursing amongst the Vietnamese.

She joined the University Settlement and she was in the offices that we occupied, and she was sitting there and Arnold Issenman, one of the three Concordia heads, was sitting here and he looked at her, and he said, "Claire, is that you?"

And she said, "Yes, it is me."

He said, "What are you doing here? What are you doing here, Claire?"

And she looked at him and she said, "Arnold, what are you doing here?"

So we were all carted away and taken to jail and photographed and fingerprinted and so on. That was that, and then we were released in the middle of the night. The charge was public mischief. Public mischief is a very serious charge. You can go to jail up to five years. We were tried in groups. We got ourselves a very good lawyer, Bernard Mergler. He was a leading left-wing lawyer in Montreal, and he assigned a young Francophone lawyer who worked very collaboratively with us to work out the defence.

The first batch were all Anglophones, and we chose to have our trial in French.

FA: Did your group speak French?

DR: Some of them did. But we chose to have our trial in French because that was the ethos of the times and a matter of principle in Québec.

The jury found us not guilty. Our records were erased.

Before we did the occupation, we tried a number of other things. After the trial, we asked ourselves, "Well, where do we go from here?" We were completely blocked because, at that infamous Concordia press conference in 1968, not only did they have that maquette that is in the archives of the CCA, but the premier of Quebec was there, Robert Bourassa, and the mayor of Montreal. A whole bunch of creatures were there from the establishment, and they thought this was wonderful. It should go forward as soon as possible.

The trial had a few paragraphs in *La Presse*, one of the dailies at the time. The English-language media did not cover it. As a matter of fact, the main daily the *Montreal Star* had a real split in it, at the editorial page. Some supported the project, some were opposed to the project. At the journalist level, they were opposed to the project.

They also didn't want to cover it because they didn't want an example of a protest of that nature that got away with it by getting a jury to say not guilty. They didn't want to spread the good news, you see?

So it wasn't covered, and we came to a dead-end. By 1973, we were all wiped out. As a matter of fact, it was quite depressing. One of our members, a young activist, actually committed suicide. Everybody scattered.

But Lucia just didn't want to give up. She said, "There must be some way of getting around it."

What we did was, and this is very interesting and very important, we decided to rebuild the community movement by not talking about housing at all. We started talking about traffic. Jeanne-Mance, for example, was a heavily trafficked road. Because they were preparing the building of their skyscraper, their towers, they wanted to redesign the sidewalks and make them more boulevard-type sidewalks, and they wanted to reduce the traffic on Parc Avenue. They turned a residential street into a major thoroughfare and just completely reconfigured the traffic flow. We found that very objectionable, and we organized street committees that engaged in all sorts of protests to reduce the traffic on streets, to put in traffic lights, and a whole bunch of things.

As people were getting together, we had a lunch sit-down at the corner of Milton and Jeanne-Mance. We blocked traffic and so on. People got to know each other again, talk, and eventually the seed of housing came up again. And that's when Lucia said, "You know, we have to try again."

I said, "Lucia, forget it. We've lost that battle. Let's do something else."

"No."

To make a long story short, as you know, she went to see Nuremberg with Michael Fish or James McGregor—one of the two—and he said, "Make me an offer."

Every major confrontation that we had really came to a head in the municipal election of 1978. We were psychologically strengthened by the support that we would get. In that renewed culture emerged the desire to go back to the original vision of constructing a co-operative society and a co-operative project.

The idea of saving heritage neighbourhoods was a radical new idea. The first person who talked that way was, of course, Lucia; and the first person who understood that idea was Phyllis Lambert.

When she walked around Milton-Parc and she saw what was there, she said, "It doesn't make sense. It would be horrible. It would be a crime to demolish a neighbourhood like this."

There was a kind of symbiotic relationship that was established between these two women. One having all the skills of organizing people and community organizing and explaining things to people, and the other looking at it from the outside in.

And then we had a scorpion that came out of a dark corner in the neighbourhood. A kind of a Fifth Column which was called Maisons Saint-Louis.

FA: That is the people who wanted to own?

DR: Yes. They started organizing. And we had to fight them. I was sort of the main strategist fighting them. Just marginalizing them. That is where the vision, the old vision of a co-operative society and a co-operative project, started coming forward again. But how to do that in a society that is based on market capitalism? That is where people like Robert Cohen and François Frenette, the famous notary, worked out the idea of this condominium for social purposes, which in English we call a land trust. In French it is called a *fiducie foncière communautaire*.

We've taken six blocks of downtown in the second biggest city in Canada. Six city blocks in downtown Montreal off the capitalist market. Do you understand what that means? It has never been done before. We have socialized the soil.

We should be very proud of that achievement. Hopefully it can happen elsewhere. That's what's unique about Milton-Parc. Not because it's all these co-ops working together, it's actually that we control the land. It belongs to the people for goodness sake

FA: And that ensures the longevity of this, too. That's what's critical.

DR: Absolutely. Academics—major writers like Saskia Sassen, Peter Marcuse, came up here and said, "You actually did this?"

And you know, there's nothing more sacred in law than the divine right to own property and the divine right of private property. Not here. Not on this street that you're walking on.

But it was a hard fight. One of the remarkable things in this story is that Phyllis Lambert understood that. Given who she was and her whole background, you would say, "Well, you know, can such a person understand any of these things?" But she understood it and she supported it straight down the line. As did Robert Cohen. Straight down the line.

And it was very important also for Canada Mortgage and Housing Corporation (CMHC), in the end, because to them it was easier to go forward with a project that had an organic integrity to it. What they wanted, of course, was to have a project that had housing that respected market rents. That was another big battle. I had a long talk with the head of the Parti Quebecois, René Lévesque, and being who he was, he said, "Look, Dimitri, if Ottawa doesn't support you, we will support you. We're going to be the next government. We will support you."

They were beginning negotiations on this whole question of the interest rate for the mortgages, which would affect this question of market rents, with the CMHC brass, and the negotiations were not going well. At one point, our people said, "Well, you know, if you're not prepared to do that, there are other levels of government who would be prepared to support us and, as a matter of fact, there are people meeting, preparing a press conference to say that Ottawa, CMHC, has put our back against the wall and insisted on something that is completely unacceptable to the community, which would drive people away. They would undermine the integrity of the project, and they are preparing a press conference to say exactly that."

Within a couple of hours, a black limousine drives up from Ottawa and the big brass come in and they say, "What is that you want?" "We want this." "Done." It's called blackmail. Creative blackmail.

FA: Was there actually a group of people preparing the press conference?

DR: There was. I was in the upstairs room talking about organizing the press conference. Oh, absolutely.

FA: Did you hope and expect the Milton-Parc example would be followed elsewhere?

DR: Yes, but let me say one other thing about the Milton-Parc project, which is very important to stress in my view. Rather than having one big co-op, like in other cities like Toronto or New York, where you have an annual meeting of eight hundred people—forget it. People formed co-ops here on the basis of affinity. They like each other or they want to be neighbours. They want to work together through a co-op. And there should be a whole bunch of them. The result is that the Communauté Milton-Parc is a federation of 16 co-ops and five non-profit housing associations, and that's important because that allows a form of participation in management which you could not possibly have if it's on a bigger scale.

Not that it's ideal, because that too—small is beautiful—has problems with it. But it doesn't have the kinds of problems that you have if you have one big outfit.

Because the whole project is on a land trust, and a land trust is—no matter how you shake it—a non-profit project, we have a privileged position in terms of paying reduced municipal taxes. This is a very sharp bone in the throats of the municipal government. Our constitution in this country is so reactionary, which gives all authority over cities to provincial governments. Our cities don't even exist in law. They're committed by the provincial legislatures. They're so dependent on property taxes, and the municipal administrations up until now have been so gutless in raising the need. In those days the dependency on property taxes was even heavier than it is now.

A few years after Milton-Parc, once everything was put in place, a second neighbourhood rose up in protest, again driven by young people. A neighbourhood which is at the corner of Rene Levesque and Guy street, downtown Montreal, a neighbourhood called Overdale. Again heritage buildings and the rest of that. And the people there put up a very valiant fight and we helped them. We'd attend their meetings, teach them how we did it, and so on and so forth. We worked really well together.

But they were arrested. Oh, that's a whole unhappy story. They were arrested, they had a trial, their trial did not succeed, and they were broken. The people who were in power at City Hall were people on the so-called left. The Montreal Citizens' Movement. Jean Doré. So-called progressives, including people who had worked in the Milton-Parc project.

They supported a big project by developers. They said, "We need the property revenue. We'll place these people somewhere else."

"They don't want to move anywhere else! This is their neighbourhood! They want to recycle these buildings. They have the right. We founded that right!"

"Can't do it."

Anyways, it's a whole tragic story itself. So that was the first immediate consequence of Milton-Parc. Didn't work. And that's the irony. You can't trust people with power, whatever their ideological colouration is.

There was a second rate attempt to do something like Milton-Parc, which is called Benny Farm in west Notre-Dame-de-Grâce, where there was a very large piece of land on which there were buildings that were built after the Second World War to house veterans. There was a big community swelling with interest to acquire the land, acquire the buildings, and turn them into a Milton-Parc number two.

It was Canada Lands because it was federal land to begin with. They did not want to have a land trust. They didn't even want to have all the housing co-operatives, and there was an enormous amount of compromising and a certain amount of skulduggery. We were told by some people, "Well, times have changed. It's not the same time."

There was division in the leadership, so Benny Farm was a very compromised project. There are some co-ops, there's some private property under certain conditions. It's a mixed bag, and I just got a report from somebody who's very much active in tenants' rights. A very dear friend of mine who monitors these situations. He says, "There are all sorts of conflicts and things going on there that would make you unhappy, Dimitri."

Somebody across the street owns their house, somebody on this street lives in a non-profit housing corporation, and somebody over there lives in a co-op. What's going to happen in terms of a community dynamic?

FA: What do you think was the critical difference that made Milton-Parc succeed where these others didn't?

DR: It's leadership and historical circumstances. Leadership can only go so far, but circumstances have to be favourable. They can be favourable in-and-of themselves, but historical circumstances can also be manipulated by the right leadership. You create history, too; you're not just a victim of history.

There was also a common vision that the core group was in entire agreement.

The only thing on which we really did not agree is that I insisted that there had to be an ongoing, highly developed community education program.

I kept saying to people, we are not born democrats. We don't come out of our mother's womb knowing what it is to attend a membership meeting and what a resolution is, and we don't understand how democracy functions at the local level or any level. We have to learn it. We can learn it from each other, we can learn it from books to a certain extent. We learn from each other. We have to go through how a board of directors functions democratically.

Our co-op, for example, is the biggest co-op. The Milton-Parc Co-op. We have an extremely democratic constitution. Everything is at the level of the general assembly, and we have functioning committees. Our level of participation is very high. I mean, people disagree and there's small-mindedness. All of that. We're deformed by our society, we cannot wash our society entirely off, like walking into a shower. But it functions very well. I would dare say, of all of the co-ops in Milton-Parc, it's the best functioning one. It's the biggest one, and it just works well.

But that takes what the women's liberation movement called consciousness-raising, what you and I can call popular education or community education. You have to have an ongoing educational program. You have to remember your history. That's what I hope about next year, 2018, reminding people of the history and sacrifices. People from the outside think, "What you've done is remarkable."
FA: Do you think there's a serious risk of the Milton-Parc spirit being lost?
DR: No, because we still have the Milton-Parc Citizens' Committee.

We're trying to release from the black bag the whole notion of self-consciousness and learning from each other and what community really means. It's not enough to overuse the term, and I am a particular stickler about how it's used because I have an enormous respect for what it means authentically. When some businessman tells me, "The business community—", I say, "There's no such thing as the business community. You're a glass jar in which there are vipers. The lid may be open or not, but don't call yourself a community. You're not a community. You're a bunch of self-interested people, for heaven's sake. Why don't you just admit it? You're interested in one thing."

I remember we had a big party two years ago at the Strathearn Centre, on Jeanne-Mance Street, which was the primary school and is now a big multi-cultural centre with all sorts of community organizations and non-profit organizations on various floors. The entire ground floor—the theatre, the café, and the gallery—was given to the Milton-Parc Citizens' Committee for free to celebrate Lucia's 80th birthday. Her surprise birthday party. There were two hundred people. It was a potluck, and community artists were there. The provincial member of Parliament, Jacques Chagnon gave a very sincere speech because he supported the project way back when and he helped pilot the private member's bill that went through the National Assembly to allow the land trust to be created. He made a statement in Lucia's honour and said, "You know, I'm a member of Parliament, but your democracy works better than ours. It's remarkable, this project. All these decades."

And I think he was sincere. There was no reason for him to butter us up for anything. So here is a very establishment figure saying this kind of thing, and yet, you see the municipal authorities are afraid of Milton-Parc. They don't want it to be duplicated. They didn't want it at Benny Farm. They colluded with the federal agency that owned that land. They didn't want Benny Farm. They didn't want Overdale. They don't want the healthy bacteria of Milton-Parc to spread, which is very unfortunate.

Lucia Kowaluk in Conversation

Editor's Note: The following is an amalgam of two interviews with Lucia Kowaluk. One interview was conducted by Francesca Ammon, Assistant Professor of City and Regional Planning at the University of Pennsylvania School of Design, took place on March 21, 2017, at Lucia's home in Co-opérative d'habitation Milton-Parc, which was part of a research project Ammon undertook for the Canadian Centre for Architecture's Multidisciplinary Research Program: Architecture and/for Photography, entitled "Captioning Milton-Parc." The other was conducted by Josh Hawley on November 17, 2017, at the Centre hospitalier de l'Université de Montréal in downtown Montreal. Excerpts from Josh Hawley's interview are italicized for clarity.

Francesca Ammon: Can you tell me a little bit about your own personal experience of the formation of the co-op that you are in?

Lucia Kowaluk: I learned that money was available to form co-operatives and it became clear that Concordia Estates Ltd. wanted to get rid of the buildings, but I didn't know what it would cost, of course. I got a grant of $2,000 from Heritage Montreal, which at the time was a lot of money, to do the research. I went down to City Hall, which was fascinating because all the old deeds were there of who lived where. That's when I realized after the war, this ceased to be a bourgeois neighbourhood and became a working-class neighbourhood and the people—the French-Canadians who lived down below and this whole line around Milton-Parc—all worked at the Hôtel-Dieu.

  I did a lot of door-knocking to see, "Would you be interested in being part of a co-operative? Would you be interested?"

  In the meantime, Paxmil sold what was left of the property to a guy named Harry Mendelsohn, who ran a pawn shop on Craig Street. And Phyllis Lambert, at that point, was beginning to feel her wings. She was becoming comfortable in Montreal and interested in these issues, more involved. She went to Mendelsohn and used her weight the way she can when she wants to and convinced him to sell to Canada Mortgage and Housing Corporation (CMHC), because through the Bronfman line of friendship, the cabinet and Prime Minister Pierre Trudeau himself were convinced this was a good project. And CMHC bought the stuff. Phyllis convinced Mendelsohn to sell for only $5.5 million.

FA: A modest profit.

LK: Whereas he was planning probably to sell off one-by-one and make piles and piles of money. Phyllis convinced him not to.

FA: And that was when Heritage Montreal really got involved?

LK: Well, it's more that Phyllis Lambert got involved. I wouldn't say Heritage Montreal, as an organization, and its board of directors was particularly involved, but Phyllis was.

When I teach community organizing at the McGill School of Social Work, I say a number of things. One is that this is a lifetime job. People who say, "We've been doing it for ten years," I say it's nothing. It took us 20 years to even get Milton-Parc off the ground. Come on. So you're in this for life or you're in this for the long haul.

Number two, you need a lot of activity on the ground. Civil activity. People. Residents. Transit people. Whatever. But people on the ground.

Another thing that you need is to understand what's happening to the economy at that particular moment. The economy was on our side. In other words, the reason Concordia Estates Ltd. couldn't do the whole project was that, from the Oil Crisis of 1972–73, we had a huge jump in inflation and the money Concordia Estates had put aside wasn't enough.

And the fourth thing is you need people in high places. The side comment to that is: don't believe that you have no access to high places. You can develop them. You start with your City Councillor. You go to your Member of Parliament. You go to your Member of the National Assembly. You talk to people. You can develop contacts with people in high places.

Our housing co-op, Co-op Milton-Parc, was the first, and the base of it was the people who had been active in the street committee. And it wasn't hard to form at all.

FA: Because you already were on the same page?

LK: We were all on the same page. We knew what a co-op was, we knew how to do it—we had knowledgeable people. I believe we are the most democratically functioning co-op in the whole project. At the very beginning, our bylaws were such that we insisted that only the general assembly could make any real, any serious decisions, and that goes against the law on co-operatives of the province. The province gives the right to the board to make some policy decisions. As co-ops go, our co-ops are small. The biggest co-ops in Quebec are the huge dairy and farmers' co-ops, with thousands of members. So, for them, it makes sense that a board can make decisions. But it did not make sense for these small groups. It's part of our bylaws that things have to go to the general assembly.

We have a schedule. The general assembly meets six times a year, and that includes the annual meeting. When co-ops say, "No, we only have a general assembly when we have something to discuss," my answer always is, "It's too late." Our bylaw and our membership contract says that you cannot miss a general assembly without a valid excuse.

Josh Hawley: The board is limited in its decision-making capabilities?
LK: Yes. For example, the board cannot make a decision on spending. In fact, there was a special meeting the other evening. It involved the expenditure of $5,000 or $6,000 to fix the front facade. There was a meeting just on that issue. Now people could say, "Nah, who wants to go out on Monday night." But people know, if they don't go, it might be voted down and nobody wanted it to be voted down. So there's that rule. The other thing is that all minutes of committee meetings, boring as they are, have to be distributed in both languages, to everybody.

The co-ops that are functioning badly are lazy. Not only are they lazy, they have little cliques. They have allowed little power cliques to form. That's always a mistake. How do you avoid that? By saying there have to be minutes every time a committee meets. There have to be minutes and those minutes have to be distributed.

The co-operative law from Quebec City says the minutes of the board should be private. We didn't agree. If the government should ever come to us, we would say, "Sorry." Now we do agree that you don't mention names if people are behind in rent, for example. Which is something very personal.

JH: *How big is your board?*
LK: Seven. We have seven committees. A member from each committee makes up the board. Then the board decides who will be the president or whatever. Committees have to meet, they have to have minutes and they have to distribute those minutes.
JH: *And every co-op member has to serve on a committee?*
LK: Every member has to be on a committee, yes.
JH: *How long were you on the board of the Communauté Milton-Parc (CMP)?*
LK: Two or three years. There is a general assembly for the CMP. The structure is such that every co-op has a seat on a general assembly. There are 15 co-ops and six non-profit housing organizations and each one has a seat. They have weighted votes. In other words, Co-op Milton-Parc is the biggest co-op and, even though there is only one person representing us, when we vote in the general assembly, the Milton-Parc vote is heavier. Our vote means more than small little co-ops or non-profits.
JH: *Do you think size has anything to do with the functioning of a housing co-op? Some co-ops, and this is common in Ontario, are a hundred units at least. Hundreds*

of units sometimes—apartments and townhouses. There are so many properties to manage and they end up bringing in a property manager to run it, and then fraud can happen and cliques form. This pattern is repeated over and over again.

LK: I remember in the years we were founding this whole project, there was an individual who was part of the Technical Resource Group, who has a real commitment to democratic functioning. He did a superb job of pulling things together for quite a few years. He's a true believer. And he doesn't live in the area, he never did. Bob Cohen is his name.

JH: Participation is key to that?

LK: Yes.

JH: The CMP has such a variety of co-ops. You must see it all from all angles. That is the kind of insight the CMP has that really no other co-op housing project has. You are able to see how some co-ops have tended more towards functioning autonomously and how other ones have really—

LK: Let it drop. It is too bad. How do you avoid it? I don't know. That's a big question. In our co-op, we have hung on to democratic functioning for a couple of reasons. It's written in our bylaws. We're fanatical in our bylaws for what has to go through the general assembly.

I can say one thing, and that is that it is a constant struggle to keep a co-op democratically run. People have to be pushed to be democratic. They have to be pushed to understand they have a sense of responsibility, that they are landlords as well as tenants. And if they don't do that, they're going to lose control. And then they're going to get bitter. And then little fights start. That's a constant danger in a co-op. Then everybody's sorry when it finally falls apart. Or, the co-op is reduced to finding outside commercial help. And I think that's too bad.

JH: It's not to say that is an inevitability, but it's a real risk.

LK: Exactly. That's very well put.

FA: What is the process for a new resident to move in?

LK: People have to go to the central office of CMP. There's a part-time manager who does mechanical things. A person or a family who wants to live here has to get the email addresses for all of the co-ops. The person can use the same letter, but the person has to send it individually to every co-op. In my own co-op, we keep applications for two years only, and then we throw them out.

FA: So people apply whether there are openings or not?

LK: That's right. They're contacted for the size.

FA: I see. So, after two years, if nothing has opened up then—

LK: That's right, it gets thrown away.

FA: As time has gone on, have there been any changes to how the co-ops were established and how they function today?

LK: There are some co-ops that have functioned very badly, and it's something that concerns me a lot. When I was on the board of CMP for a few of years, I undertook to go around and meet with co-ops and talk to their boards. I did a little bit of it, but very little. I was busy and, I didn't do what I said I would do. There's a need for that.

We should also talk about how the non-profits are run. There are two types of non-profits in Milton-Parc. What happened is that the Maisons Saint-Louis people, who were in favour of buying their own properties, would be damned if they would be a co-op when they lost that fight, and so they formed two non-profits and they don't run democratically. But there are three that were originally meant to be non-profits: 55/65, Yellow Door, and Chambrelle.

Then a fourth one, Chambreclerc, was founded by me when I ran the drop-in at Saint James United Church for homeless people. So at that time, someone gave up two pieces of land where there had been an old, old fire; so those two pieces of land are Chambreclerc. And those are rooming houses with two communal kitchens in each building.

But Chambrelle is the one that really bugs me. That's a long story. God. The guy who was working there defrauded $40,000 and CMHC required the board to just put the rents way up. So now they have these high, high rents, and they're full of students, and that was not the intention. That's a mess that we have to sort out. It's really too bad that happened.

There are still a lot of people of good will. But there's still a lot of people, new people who come in, who don't participate. They don't have a copy of the Milton-Parc guidebook.

It took me about five years to write that book. There was a lack of information among new members about co-ops and their history. There were people in my own co-op, as an example, who didn't know who Phyllis Lambert was.

FA: So there are certain obligations to history, to the way that Milton-Parc functions.

LK: Yes, that's right. So, recently, because the selection committee did not do a good job of bringing people up-to-date, and giving them a history, and forcing them to do certain things, and learning about stuff, that they have to sit on a committee, and that they have to give a minimum of six hours a month to the co-op and so forth… Luckily we still have enough old members still living here who remember the old rules.

That is an example of how we function now. It could be a lot better and we should have more rules about taking new members in and informing them. And it should be better run, and Chambrelle should be adjusted for people with very, very low incomes who need rooms, and not students who are rich. But you can't do everything.

JH: Why were co-ops chosen in the first place? The battle started as a fight for housing and to prevent displacement of the people who were there. Then co-ops only came as an idea later on. It was like a tool or a technique. How did co-ops come to be that tool?
LK: Well that's the history of co-operatives, based on the Rochdale principles that came out of England in the early part of the 19th Century. Those were people who believed in those values. Bob Cohen convened meetings for several years, let me tell you. Every week we met and decided on everything. But we looked at those Rochdale principles. One of the things we decided on was following those principles.

We knew we wanted to have democratic functioning and we spent hours deciding on principles that went into the CMP's Declaration of Co-ownership. We were trapped because the rules governing co-ops in Quebec did not necessarily suffice. Bob Cohen tracked down a man named François Frenette who was a notary and has been known to have said the proudest thing in his life was Milton-Parc.

What Frenette did was use condominium law, because co-op law allowed too much autonomy to the board, which we didn't agree with. Whereas condominium law actually is more inherently democratic. It's amazing, in fact. If you buy a condominium in a complex, you have all kinds of rights. And you not only have rights, but you have the right to make restrictions. "You may not have dogs that bark after eleven o'clock," for example. There's no other group of laws governing living which allows the conglomerate, or the community, to make those kinds of rules. The other big one is we couldn't resell. In our capitalist society, you cannot forbid people from alienating property. You can't do that. You can't prevent them from reselling.
JH: But you managed to do that with Milton-Parc.
LK: We did it because we used condominium law. There's enough in it that allowed us to make restrictions. We also made restrictions on who could live there in the sense of income. That all fell into place and became the Declaration of Co-ownership. It was exactly what we wanted.
JH: You needed the sort of abstract notions of democracy and participation. However, those can easily lead to any decisions being made that may not have a class awareness or be anti-capitalist. You can easily have a democratic process in a capitalist society.
LK: Yes.
JH: But Milton-Parc was able to take the housing off the market and ensure that it stays off the market and any decisions made along the way are co-operative.
LK: That's right. It's quite amazing. It's quite an amazing project.
JH: A lot of housing co-ops elsewhere are missing the politics behind them. They should be celebrating their goal of keeping housing off the market. That's why housing co-ops exist.
LK: Yes, that's right. It's no wonder Dimitri goes around the world bragging about Milton-Parc. It's unique.

There was a member of one of the co-ops who tried to undo the Declaration of Co-ownership. She wanted to challenge it. There are myths going around the CMP that when the mortgage is up, people can buy their houses. They haven't read the Declaration.

This one member brought in a well-known notary to analyze the Declaration of Co-ownership and to see whether there was a loophole where once the mortgage was over we could sell our property. She was sure this notary would show ways in which people could buy their property but it didn't go her way. The notary ended up having so much fun defending the Declaration and at the end he said Frenette, who drafted the Declaration, did a magnificent job.

JH: It is rock solid.

LK: Rock solid. Absolutely rock solid.

JH: Are evictions rare in your co-op?

LK: Yes, very rare. Very, very rare.

JH: And so residents never feel like they have nowhere to turn? In Ontario, for example, residents of co-ops don't have access to the Landlord and Tenant Board because they're not considered tenants. They're considered members of a private group. When co-op evictions have gone to court, the precedent has been set by certain judges saying these residents are part of private clubs, like a gentlemen's club.

LK: No, because they're protected by the rental board in Quebec. For example, there was a member in my co-op, who made a mess of things. He was supposed to be the secretary and he left all the archives out in the rain because he was pissed off nobody came and collected them. He was expelled as a member. And he had the right in front of the rental board of keeping his house. In fact, he just recently left.

JH: If it wasn't for the co-op movement, there wouldn't be all this housing, this low-rent, subsidized housing. And good quality housing for the most part.

LK: Yes. Have you been in our house? Isn't it gorgeous? Imagine that being smashed down. Of course not all co-ops, especially new co-ops, are beautiful like that. It's because we're living in old houses. And CMHC subsidized the renovation of them, which was expensive.

JH: My thought is that Milton-Parc got away with what it did because it was able to catch CMHC off guard. You outsmarted them. But now they are wise to it. CMHC is now even trying to push co-ops, even those in Milton-Parc, to approach market rent. I wonder if something like Milton-Parc could ever happen again in Canada. You can't follow the model because there are no best practices, but there are a lot of lessons to be learned.

LK: It's a very good question. Thank God for the Declaration of Co-ownership, because it prevents us from raising the rents. The Declaration of Co-ownership says we have to rent to people of low and middle-income.

JH: There's a lot of talk now about community land trusts (CLTs). The people from the Champlain Housing Trust in Vermont, the largest CLT in the United States, even came to Milton-Parc to learn from it in the 1980s and again a few years ago. It seems like what was done here was to create a type of land trust.

LK: Yes. That's another item of course. I think the existence of our land trust is because, again, we fought for it. In fact, when we tried to do it for Benny Farm, the City of Montreal wouldn't go for it. Because they knew our municipal taxes for the CMP are low, on top of everything else.

JH: So the City is angry they are missing out on all of that potential tax revenue.

LK: That's right. Boy, are we lucky. No wonder people are dying to get into the Milton-Parc co-ops.

We also have acquired rights. The Declaration of Co-ownership would not allow me to live in that big house now if there wasn't acquired rights. It's no wonder we have the time and energy to be volunteers.

JH: Because you have secure housing.

LK: Yeah. Our house is huge, but we give back a lot. There have been a number of projects that wanted to copy Milton-Parc and were not able to. They didn't get the support from the City. Well, because it's just too good a deal.

JH: There are always little battles to be fought and those are still important. Saving a park, adding bike lanes, calming traffic, stuff like that. But housing is still the fundamental issue. Everything revolves around housing and land. So if this issue is mainly solved, is it important to still have that politicization?

LK: Well I think so. There are a handful of people who do come out of the woodwork. There are good people around. For one thing, it's fun. I think there are individuals in our society who just love doing this kind of thing. It gives them the opportunity. But there are dozens who do very little.

There are a lot of people in the co-ops who, having this good housing, take jobs which are low paid and socially useful. I would say there are probably more people like that than not. A lot of that comes from the selection committee.

On the whole, the people in my co-op understand they are living in good housing and so they have some responsibility to give back. The husband of a family we recently accepted now works at the legal clinic in Pointe-St-Charles at a minimum wage. He's a really good guy. There's another guy who, now that he just finished his PhD thesis, is talking about what he can do in the community. It allows people to blossom.

JH: The redevelopment of the Hôtel Dieu, which is located right next door to Milton-Parc, is going to be a big project. How likely do you think it is the Communauté Saint-Urbain, of which the CMP is a member, is successful in converting it to housing?

LK: It's full of recently renovated large comfortable rooms. Homeless people, poor, elderly, all kinds of people could live in that housing. It could be a wonderful project.

I can picture the relationship between an elderly person and a family. The elderly person could help out with babysitting and people could enjoy the summer together or the winter together... The vision is so clear in my mind.

JH: *It seems like a once in-a-lifetime project. When is a property like that ever going to be available again?*

LK: *Exactly, exactly. Very much so. When else is it going to be available? Phyllis Lambert is the Communauté Saint-Urbain's honorary president. I'd be happy to name the whole bloody thing after her.*

JH: *It does seem like the perfect project. It seems like the Communauté Saint-Urbain project is like a natural sequel to Milton-Parc. Do you think it could be like the way Milton-Parc happened?*

LK: *You know what? In my head, if I wasn't sick, I was ready to organize a sit-in. And say, "OK people, now's the time to act on this project." There are two big parking lots going all the way down to Sherbrooke. All of those should have housing on them. That would bring a big jump in the demographics and just plain money. People don't realize—just plain money. I mean two thousand families living on the west side of Saint Urbain can bring money into Saint Laurent boulevard for heaven's sake, which is half dead. Anyway, I don't know if I'll ever be able to do those things again. There are more than a few organizations already involved so I'm encouraged.*

LK (*continued from FA interview*): It really does take a vision that this makes sense, and then you just have to keep going on that vision. I'm the same now with the Hôtel Dieu Hospital. I know we have to win something because it doesn't make sense. What else are they going to do with that building, which they can't touch because it's a heritage thing? What else are they going to do? Once that's clear to me, then I just keep doing it. I just keep doing it.

Appendix A: Financial and Technical Participation of CMHC in Milton-Parc

Editor's Note: This list is adapted from the September 23, 1983 press release issued by CMHC to celebrate the inauguration of Milton-Parc.

Financial and Technical Participation of CMHC

1979
- The Canadian government, through CMHC, invests $5.5 million under article 55 of the National Housing Act to buy the 506 dwellings, 132 rooms and 20 businesses that make up Milton-Parc. This government gesture would make neighbourhood organization into co-ops and non-profit groups possible.

1980
- CMHC resells these properties to the Société d'Amélioration Milton-Parc, with a balance on the selling price and other charges amounting to nearly $7 million.
- CMHC guarantees 100% of mortgage loans allowing for the purchase of homes.
- National Housing Act article 6—$24,310,000
- CMHC grants a start-up fund, not to be reimbursed, which helps to set up co-ops and non-profit groups.
- National Housing Act article 37.1—$87,500
- CMHC gives grants to technical resource groups, as part of the community resources organization program, up to May 1983.
- National Housing Act article 36G—$770,000
- CMHC gives another grant, following Part 5 of the National Housing Act, designed to support the application of new housing concepts helping to improve the housing and living conditions of Canadians.
- National Housing Act part 5—$306,670
- Following article 56.1 of the National Housing Act, CMHC commits itself to

a grant guaranteeing the maintenance of rents at a reasonable cost. This grant, taking the form of an interest-rate rebate equivalent to 2% financing, will cost $3,966,000 per year for the first five years. After that it will be readjusted, according to the interest rates, for each mortgage renewal.
- CMHC has also given grants for renovations, based on the number of housing units renovated, under the Canadian Home Renovation Program.
- National Housing Act article 34.1—$2,185,000

Appendix B:
Timeline of Milton-Parc: 1979-1987

Editor's Note: This timeline is adapted from an unauthored document found in the Milton-Parc archives housed at the Canadian Centre for Architecture. Dates and events have been added to this timeline from other two other sources: Milton-Parc: How We Did It and How It Works Now, and the 30th anniversary calendar issued by the Communauté Milton-Parc in 2018.

Timeline of Milton-Parc, 1979-1987

January 1979
The residents of the Milton-Parc neighbourhood ask Heritage Montreal to engage the federal government.

May 1979
CMHC purchases the properties with the promise to sell to the non-profit corporation Société du Patrimoine Urbain de Montréal (SPUM) which has a mandate to realize the Milton-Parc project.

May–June 1979
The first five permanent employees and four summer students are hired by SPUM (which consisted of a total of 21 people).

June 1979
The community holds a general assembly to explain the project.

August 1979
Founding of Co-op Milton-Parc.

Summer 1979
Preliminary surveys are done for all buildings.
SPUM and community members prepare the Action Plan with help from the Conseil de Développement du Logement Communautaire (CDLC).

The Federation of Co-operatives of Milton-Parc is created, which later becomes the Conseil Milton-Parc.

October 1979
The Action Plan is adopted by the residents of the neighbourhood following a community assembly.
The Milton-Parc Technical Resource Group, Inc. is formed.

November 1979
A negotiating committee is formed to ensure the financial viability and, specifically, that rents are kept low after renovations.

November 1979–May 1980
Negotiations with CMHC take place to ensure the financial viability of the project.

Winter 1980
The City of Montreal agrees to ensure access to municipal restoration programs and financial support from the City.

January 1980
Founding of co-ops Sainte-Famille, Concerto, Du Nordet, and La Petite Cité.

March 1980
The first authorization request to sell the properties from CMHC to the community is made to the Régie du Logement.
Founding of co-ops La Tour des Alentours and Du Chez-Soi.

May 1980
An agreement with CMHC is made on the rents after renovations. This agreement recognizes the right of occupants to return to their units after the renovations and to pay an affordable rent.

June 1980
Founding of Co-op Les Tourelles and non-profit housing organizations Porte Jaune and 55/65.

September 1980
CMHC accepts the sale of the properties to an organization affiliated with

SPUM, the Société d'Amélioration Milton-Parc (SAMP), and ensures that each co-op and non-profit will be financially independent from one another.

October 1980
CMHC sells the properties to SAMP, which now becomes the landlord for all the buildings.
Renovations begin for Co-op Milton-Parc and Co-op Du Nordet.
A number of residents who thought they could buy titles to the individual buildings in which they live withdraw their demands.

Fall 1980
A research committee is formed to create management contracts for each co-op and non-profit.

December 1980
Renovations begin for Co-op Petite Cité and Phase 1 of Co-op Sainte-Famille.

March 1981
Reintegration of residents into the first units that were renovated.
Renovations begin for Co-op Porte Jaune.

April 1981
Renovations begin for Co-op La Tour des Alentours.
Founding of non-profit housing organization Village Jeanne-Mance.

Spring 1981
Distribution of a project evaluation questionnaire to the co-ops and non-profits.
Creation of a research committee to outline the conditions of sale for all properties in Milton-Parc.

May 1981
Renovations begin for the non-profit Société D'Habitation 55/65 de la Rue Jeanne-Mance.

June 1981
The co-ops and non-profits hold a seminar on the results of the evaluation questionnaire.

July 1981
A brochure is published on the conditions of sale.
Renovations begin for Co-op Les Tourelles and Phase 1 of Co-op Concerto.

August 1981
A neighbourhood business committee is created.
The community holds a general assembly to discuss the question of the conditions of sale.
Founding of non-profit housing organization Allegro.

October 1981
Renovations begin for Co-op Du Chez-Soi.
Founding of Co-op Rue des Artistes.

Fall 1981
The research committee begins work on the financial model for the neighbourhood to ensure a distribution of potential surpluses amongst the co-ops and non-profits, which would result in affordable rent for all.

December 1981
Founding of Co-op L'Escale.

February 1982
Renovations begin for Phase 2 of Co-op Sainte-Famille.

May 1982
The co-ops and non-profits decide to create a non-profit organization to manage the commercial properties.
Renovations begin for non-profit Société d'Habitation Village Jeanne-Mance.

June 1982
Founding of the Co-op L'Alliance.

July 1982
Founding of Co-op Petite Hutchison.

August 1982
Renovations begin for Co-op Rue des Artistes.

September 1982
Renovations begin for Co-op La Petite Hutchison, Phase 2 of Co-op Concerto, and the non-profit Société d'Habitation Allegro.
Founding of co-ops Les Colonnes and Les Jardins.

Fall 1982
An agreement is made between the City of Montreal and the Société d'Habitation du Québec (SHQ) to access Loginove, the provincial residential renovation program, for the remaining buildings.

November 1982
Renovations begin for Co-op L'Alliance.

December 1982
Renovations begin for Co-op L'Escale.

September 1985
Founding of Co-op La Voie Lactée.

April 1986
Founding of non-profit housing organization Chambrelle.

May 1986
A draft "Declaration of Co-ownership" (the Declaration), is formally presented to the community.

April 1987
Founding of non-profit housing organization Chambreclerc.

June 1987
The Declaration of Co-ownership is passed into law at the Quebec National Assembly.

August 1987
The Quebec government rules that municipal taxes for the properties owned by Communauté Milton-Parc should be based on their decreased non-market value because of the rules preventing resale for non-speculative purposes.

December 1987
SAMP signs over the deed of sale and the Declaration is signed by each co-op and non-profit. They become co-owners and the Communauté Milton-Parc begins.

About the Authors

Julien Deschênes
Julien Deschênes, a Fine Arts Core Education (F.A.C.E.) alumni, recently completed a master's in Urban Planning. As a born and raised Montrealer, he grew up a few steps away from the intersection of Sherbrooke Street and Saint-Laurent Boulevard which forged a need to understand the social fabric of the city. His interests have allowed him to focus on affordable housing created by community land trusts, specifically how public policies could accelerate such models. His involvement in social and political affairs represents a dedication towards a fairer, friendlier, and more sustainable community.

Josh Hawley
Josh Hawley's interest in Milton-Parc emerged from having spent his formative years in housing co-ops and solidified through an MA in Cultural Studies at Queen's University, which focuses on resident experiences in co-ops. Josh is involved in the battle to save his home neighbourhood of Herongate, located in Canada's capital, Ottawa. In 2018, Josh also helped co-curate the Canadian Centre for Architecture exhibition, "Milton-Parc: How We Did It."

Lucia Kowaluk
Lucia Kowaluk is a well-known community organizer and social worker. She has been credited for her antipoverty work and in establishing housing for the homeless and street people of Montreal. Recipient of many awards including the personality of the year by the FECHIMM, the leading co-operative housing federation in Quebec, Canada, the Daviau prize awarded by the City of Montreal, the Order of Canada and the Order Nationale du Quebec.

Dimitri Roussopoulos

Dimitri Roussopoulos is a community organiser, writer, public speaker, theorist and a founder of the Milton-Parc project, who has lectured widely on social housing, land trusts and urban ecology. From the 1960s to the present he has been active in the disarmament and anti-war movement, both local and internationally, and has published some 15 books, some translated into several languages.

Iman Salama

Iman Salama studied design of the environment at the University of Quebec in Montreal and urban planning at the University of Montreal. Through several years of professional experience and practice in various contexts, she learned to see cities through the prism of daily human activities and behaviours. Passionate about how people can shape their own habitats, Iman is a specialist in participatory planning processes and has worked in North America, Africa and Europe.

Brenda Torpy

Brenda Torpy has 34 years of experience in the affordable housing field, starting with rural community development and affordable housing advocacy in northern Vermont. As the Community and Economic Development Office's first Housing Director for the City of Burlington, Brenda led the development of the Burlington Community Land Trust, now Champlain Housing Trust, and served as the founding Board President. In 1991, she joined the staff as Executive Director.

The Rise of Cities: Montréal, Toronto, Vancouver and Other Cities

Dimitri Roussopoulos (ed.)
With Bill Freeman,
Patrick J. Smith, Shawn Katz
and Ann Marie Utratel

250 Pages, bibliography
Paper, $19.99/£13.99,
ISBN: 978-1-55164-334-2

Cloth, $36.99/£24.99,
ISBN: 978-1-55164-335-9

E-book, ISBN: 978-1-55164-615-2

IN THE EARLY 2000s human society entered a new urban epoch in which the majority of human beings live in cities. While the city has historically been viewed as the foundation of democracy and citizenship, the geo-political spaces of modern cities are widely misunderstood despite their key role in shaping contemporary global society. How and why have cities become the command centres of the world economy? Does globalization menace cities as we know them? Are cities able to exercise democratic control and strategic choice when multinational corporate competition increasingly limits the importance of place? *The Rise of Cities* offers intriguing responses to these questions by analyzing how cities coalesce, develop, and thrive and how they can remake themselves for better or for worse.